SpringerBriefs in Education

More information about this series at http://www.springer.com/series/8914

A. Reis Monteiro

The Teaching Profession

Present and Future

Springer

A. Reis Monteiro
University of Lisbon
Lisbon
Portugal

ISSN 2211-1921   ISSN 2211-193X   (electronic)
ISBN 978-3-319-12129-1   ISBN 978-3-319-12130-7   (eBook)
DOI 10.1007/978-3-319-12130-7

Library of Congress Control Number: 2014951725

Springer Cham Heidelberg New York Dordrecht London

For Berta and Manuel

Acknowledgments

Yong Dou (Michael) Kim, doctoral student at Villanova University (Pennsylvania), contributed with editing work for the final form of this manuscript. He deserves my deep gratitude. The contributions of two anonymous reviewers are also sincerely acknowledged, especially one who was particularly open-minded and generous. I hope that he or she does not take issue with me for quoting these lines of his or her review:

> The manuscript makes a genuine and original contribution to the field. [...]
> The author takes a strong stance and expresses a clear voice around his position, leaving no doubt about the author's unambiguous views. In doing so the manuscript is provocative and, from my point of view, this outspoken orientation is a powerful way of engaging the reader. [...]
> This manuscript should have wide appeal. It would appeal to teacher educators, to teachers with an interest in the profession, to government bodies and to members of the professional associations and to leaders of the professional associations. I hope that it is read by policy makers.

Preliminary Observations

1. There is great diversity among languages and authors concerning the use of capital or lower case letters. This text takes the following criterion: to respect, as a rule, the preferences of the quoted authors but to use capital letters for highlighting certain concepts, to distinguish certain uses of a term or to designate disciplines of knowledge.
2. When an author is cited for the first time, his or her first name is referred to in full and, if he or she is no longer alive, the dates of his or her birth and death are given in parentheses. Consecutive quotations of the same source are referenced only with page number. Notes inside quotations are suppressed, as usual, and a quotation within a quotation might be enclosed with single quotation marks. The criterion for placing a quotation in a free-standing block, without quotation marks, is rather pragmatic: it is a mix of length and importance of the text quoted.
3. Nowadays, the Internet serves as an increasingly valuable, easily accessible and frequently unavoidable documental source. In this text, when an exclusively electronic source is quoted, it is, as a rule, referred to only in footnote: without access date, if originated from an electronic site that is institutionally stable; indicating month and year of access, if the presumption of stability is uncertain. There are, however, no immortal links; their volatility is high (although it is generally possible to try to find the documents elsewhere, if they remain available online). When a document included in the references is available electronically too, its source is mentioned.

Contents

Part II   Professionality of Teachers

Part III   Self-regulation: A Bridge Between the Present and the
Future of the Teaching Profession?

Chapter 1
Introduction

Abstract Quality education is a leitmotif of political–pedagogic rhetoric, both at the international and national levels. The most decisive ingredient of education quality is the quality of the teaching profession—this is a main finding of numerous international and national reports and studies on the teaching profession and education systems published during the last three decades or so. However, another equally main finding is that the overall teachers' status, in most countries, is low or very low. How then to conceive of and achieve quality in the teaching profession? Given its degraded status and the revolution of technologies of information and communication, another issue is emerging: Does the teaching profession have a future? These and other related questions are succinctly addressed in the three parts of this volume.

Keywords Quality education · Teaching profession quality · Future of the teaching profession

Quality education is a leitmotif of political–pedagogic rhetoric, both at international and national levels. The most decisive ingredient of education quality is the quality of the teaching profession—this is a main finding of numerous international and national reports and studies on the teaching profession and education systems published during the last three decades or so. However, another equally main finding is that the overall teachers' status, in most countries, is low or very low. The reports and studies include the following:

- UNESCO (United Nations Educational, Scientific and Cultural Organization): *Learning to be: The World of Education Today and Tomorrow* (Faure Report 1972); *Learning: The Treasure Within* (Delors Report 1996); *World Education Report—Teachers and Teaching in a Changing World* (1998); *World Education Report—The Right to Education: Towards Education for all Throughout Life* (2000).
- ILO (International Labour Organization): *Handbook of good human resource practices in the teaching profession* (2012).
- World Bank: *What matters most in teacher policies?—A framework for building a more effective teaching profession* (2012).

© The Author(s) 2015
A. Reis Monteiro, *The Teaching Profession*, SpringerBriefs in Education,
DOI 10.1007/978-3-319-12130-7_1

- OECD (Organization for Economic Co-operation and Development): *Teachers Matter: Attracting, Developing and Retaining Effective Teachers* (2005); *Building a High-Quality Teaching Profession—Lessons from around the World —Background Report for the International Summit on the Teaching Profession* (2011a); *Strong Performers and Successful Reformers in Education—Lessons from PISA for the United States* (2011b); *Preparing Teachers and Developing School Leaders for the 21st Century: Lessons from around the World* (2012); *Teachers for the 21st Century—Using Evaluation to Improve Teaching— Background Report for the 2013 International Summit on the Teaching Profession* (2013); *Equity, Excellence and Inclusiveness in Education—Policy Lessons from Around the World* (2014a); *TALIS 2013 Results—An International Perspective of Teaching and Learning* (2014b).
- European Commission: *Supporting the Teaching Professions for Better Learning Outcomes* (2012).
- United States of America (USA): *Educating a Profession* (American Association of Colleges for Teacher Education 1976); *A Nation at Risk: The Imperative for Educational Reform* (National Commission on Excellence in Education 1983); *The Making of a Profession* (American Federation of Teachers 1985); *A Nation Prepared: Teachers for the 21st Century—the Report of the Task Force on Teaching as a Profession* (Carnegie Forum on Education and the Economy 1986); *Tomorrow's Teachers* (The Holmes Group 1986); *What Matters Most: Teaching for America's Future* (National Commission on Teaching and America's Future 1996); *Tough Choices or Tough Times* (National Center on Education and the Economy 2007).
- United Kingdom (UK): *The Status of Teachers and the Teaching Profession in England: Views from Inside and Outside the Profession—Final Report of the Teacher Status Project* (Hargreaves et al. 2007); *Great Teachers: Attracting, Training and Retaining the Best—Ninth Report of Session 2010–12, Volume I: Report, together with formal minutes* (House of Commons 2012).
- Australia: *A Class Act—Inquiry into the Status of the Teaching Profession* (Parliament of the Commonwealth of Australia 1998); *Quality Matters—Revitalising teaching: Critical times, critical choices* (Ramsey 2000); *Top of the Class—Report on the Inquiry into Teacher Education* (Parliament of the Commonwealth of Australia 2007).
- New Zealand: *Perceptions of Teachers and Teaching—Final Report* (Kane and Mallon 2006); *Perceptions of the Status of Teachers* (Hall and Langton 2006).
- France: *Livre Vert sur l'Évolution du Métier d'Enseignant—Rapport au Ministre de l'Éducation Nationale* (Pochard 2008); *Refondons l'École de la République—Rapport de la Concertation* (Dulot 2012).
- Other: *How the World's Best-performing School Systems Come out on Top* (Barber and Mourshed 2007); *The International Summit on the Teaching Profession—Improving Teacher Quality Around the World* (Asia Society 2011); *The 2012 International Summit on the Teaching Profession—Teaching and Leadership for the Twenty-First Century* (Asia Society 2012); *Lessons in country performance in education—2012 Report* (Pearson 2012); *Future of the*

Teaching Profession (MacBeath 2012); *The 2013 International Summit on the Teaching Profession–Teacher Quality* (Asia Society 2013); *The 2014 International Summit on the Teaching Profession—Excellence, equity, and inclusiveness—High quality teaching for all* (Asia Society 2014).

How to conceive of and reach the teaching profession quality?

Given its degraded status and the revolution of technologies of information and communication, another issue is emerging: Does the teaching profession have a future?

These and other related questions are addressed in this manuscript. It is not a literature review of the topics it addresses, nor a worldwide overview of education reforms. It draws heavily on the evidence offered by the aforementioned international and national reports and studies for submitting bold conclusions. That is why it has recourse to varied quotations, without avoiding some enlightening redundancies, and the subtitles of its second and third chapters take a rather propositional wording and tone. The approach to the teaching profession's professionality and self-regulation draws on, and updates, two studies published by this author (Monteiro 2010, 2014).

This volume only intends to be a succinct inquiry into the present and future of the teaching profession. It is structured and developed as follows:

- Part I focuses on the dialectical relationship existing between education quality and quality of the teaching profession. Two main approaches to quality education are outlined, and the principal findings of the aforementioned reports and studies are summarized. Finland is highlighted as a case study of a successful education system and highly ranked teaching profession.
- Part II discusses teachers' professionality, i.e. its global profile. It begins with a brief introduction to the Sociology of the Professions. Thereafter, the status of the teaching profession in most countries is synthesized, and some views are submitted on the vexed issue of its identity, its critical ethical dimension, the varied factors of its quality and the challenge of its future.
- Part III makes a strong case for the self-regulation of the teaching profession. After a short introduction to the field of professional regulation, an overview of the international movement towards self-regulation of the teaching profession is provided, the resistances it meets are illustrated, the benefits it brings are pointed out, and its bodies profile is described.

References

Monteiro, A. R. (2010). *Auto-regulação da Profissão Docente—Para cuidar do seu Valor e dos seus Valores* (*Self-regulation of the teaching profession—Caring about its value and values*). Braga: Associação Nacional de Professores.

Monteiro, A. R. (2014). *Profissão Docente: Profissionalidade e Auto-regulação* (*Teaching profession: Professionality and self-regulation*). São Paulo: Cortez Editora.

Part I
Education Quality and Quality of the Teaching Profession

Chapter 2
Main Approaches to Education Quality

Abstract Classic pedagogic thought is concerned with *good education*. Since the 1980s, however, *quality education* has become the watchword. What exactly is "quality" in education? We may distinguish two principal approaches: the human capital approach and the human rights approach. The human capital approach to education quality is supported by a neoliberal conception of the school's mission and of the identity of the teaching profession, based on quasi-market principles. The human rights approach to education quality is inspired by the normative content of the right to education, as internationally agreed, reflecting human rights values and principles. Quality education is a complex concept, with material and non-material dimensions, resulting from the interaction between tangible and intangible ingredients. While there is no recipe or ready-to-wear approach to producing quality education, there are principles universally valid and applicable, forming a common pedagogic heritage of Humankind amply consecrated by the Ethics of the Right to Education. In addition, every country can learn from the most exemplary ones.

Keywords Education quality · Human capital approach · Human rights approach · Complex concept

Classic pedagogic thought is concerned with *good education*. As Immanuel Kant (1724–1804) taught (1803): "It is through good education that all the good in the world arises" (p. 15). At present, *quality education* is the watchword, having become a leitmotif of political–pedagogic rhetoric, both at international and national levels.

It was only at the beginning of the 1980s that the word "quality" began to impregnate the discourse on education, under pressure from economic concerns, following the recession of the late 1970s (see OECD 1989). Nevertheless, quality

© The Author(s) 2015
A. Reis Monteiro, *The Teaching Profession*, SpringerBriefs in Education,
DOI 10.1007/978-3-319-12130-7_2

education had already been addressed by the main instrument of International Education Law[1]: the Convention against Discrimination in Education (UNESCO 1960)[2] that refers to education quality three times. For example: "For the purposes of this Convention, the term 'education' refers to all types and levels of education, and includes access to education, the standard and quality of education, and the conditions under which it is given" (Article 1.2). Also in the Recommendation concerning the Status of Teachers (ILO/UNESCO 1966)[3]—which is the main international instrument concerning basic and secondary education teachers—the word "quality" appears six times (referring to education and teachers). For example: "[A]s an educational objective, no State should be satisfied with mere quantity, but should seek also to improve quality" (10.g).

What is exactly "quality" in education?

The first United Nations Special Rapporteur on the Right to Education (Katarina Tomaševski, 1998–2004) highlighted in her Preliminary Report to the former Commission on Human Rights (E/CN.4/1999/49, para. 13)[4]:

> A definition of people as human capital obviously differs from defining people as subjects of rights. The contrast between the human rights and human-capital approaches is best illustrated by taking children with physical and learning disabilities as an example. The former may be excluded from school because providing wheelchair access, for example, might be deemed too expensive; the latter may be excluded from schooling because meeting their learning needs is deemed not to yield a sufficient marginal return on investment. This type of reasoning obviously challenges the very assumption of human rights, namely the equal worth of all human beings.

In another Report (E/CN.4/2000/6),[5] she observed: "The human-capital approach molds education solely towards economically relevant knowledge, skills and competence, to the detriment of human rights values. [...] A productivist view of education depletes it of much of its purpose and substance".

We may, therefore, distinguish two main approaches to quality education: the human capital approach and the human rights approach.

---

[1] International Human Rights Law is a new branch of the International Law, which developed after World War II, concerned with human rights. International Education Law, broadly understood, may be thus defined: it is the branch of International Human Rights Law whose scope is the right to education—its origins, normative sources, mechanisms of protection, case law, content, doctrine and political–pedagogic implications as well.

[2] http://portal.unesco.org/en/ev.php-URL_ID=12949andURL_DO=DO_TOPICandURL_SECTION=201.html.

[3] www.unesco.org/education/pdf/TEACHE_E.PDF.

[4] www.unhchr.ch/Huridocda/Huridoca.nsf/TestFrame/6a76ced2c8c9efc780256738003abbc8?Opendocument.

The mandate of Special Rapporteur is one of the extra-conventional mechanisms (*Special Procedures*), that is, not based on a treaty, created by the former United Nations Commission on Human Rights to examine, monitor and publicly report on either the human rights situation in a specific country or territory (country mandates) or on human rights violations worldwide (thematic mandates). The Commission was replaced with the Human Rights Council in 2005.

[5] http://ap.ohchr.org/documents/alldocs.aspx?doc_id=1920.

2.1   The Human Capital Approach to Education Quality Undermines Human Worth and Dignity, Tends to Dissolve the Integrity of the School Mission, and Disfigures the Uniqueness and Fullness of the Teaching Profession

The *human capital approach* originated in the human capital theory elaborated in the 1960s at the University of Chicago, especially by Gary Becker and Theodore Schultz. It is an economic approach, reducing education quality to utilitarian and quantitative indicators, regarding human beings principally as tools of economic productivity and competition. As Joel Spring (2000) remarks, the "human resource and human capital model of schooling" treats students "as a resource to be developed for the good of the economic system" (p. 148). That is the neoliberal approach.

"Neoliberalism" is a term coined by the German scholar Alexander Rüstow (1885–1963) in 1938. While, in general, it is not always well defined, the term became frequently used as a pejorative against the ideology advocating a minimal State in favour of a greater role for the private sector in the economy. Neoliberalism presents itself as an ideology of liberty and social progress but is, in reality, an economic fundamentalism of unbridled market freedom, commanding deregulation, privatization and disinvestment in public services. Its productive effectiveness is brutally destructive for human beings and their environment. It is a dictatorship of the economy, reductive of human beings to work force and consumers, their utility counting for more than their dignity. Its world is a market without borders nor scruples nor sense of the Common Good, through the weakening and submission of States. It is the drive of an "ultra-liberal financial and deregulated globalization", as an important report prepared for the French President (Védrine 2007, paras. 3 and 19) reads.

In short, neoliberalism is a *market religion* whose dogma is *competitiveness* and whose virtue is *profit*. Its dehumanizing logic is, at best, compatible with dictatorships more economically efficient than democracies. At worst, it is potentially as barbarous as Nazi biologism. Indeed, when it refers to people as "human capital" and "human resources", the neoliberal terminology carries a gloomy resonance, as Supiot (2005) remarks:

> The language of the Third Reich was the crucible of notions such 'human material' that reduce the world of human beings to that of things. […] Far from having disappeared after the war, such schemes of thought remain alive today. The talk is no more about 'human material' but about 'human capital', using, unknowingly, Stalin's vocabulary. (p. 105)

The neoliberal tide flooded the education field too. It is alleged that introducing market or quasi-market principles into the education system—privatization, competition, testing, etc.—increases its efficiency and promotes freedom of choice for families concerning the type of school wanted for their children. Such ideological views are not validated by facts, as an OECD Report (2014) concludes:

> Since the early 1980s, reforms in many countries have granted parents and students greater choice in the school the students will attend. Students and their families are given the freedom to seek and attend the school that best serves students' education needs; that, in turn, introduces a level of

competition among schools to attract students. Assuming that students and parents have all the required information about schools and choose schools based on academic criteria, the competition creates incentives for institutions to organise programmes and teach in ways that better meet diverse student requirements and interests, reducing the costs of failure and mismatches.
[…]
However, cross-country correlations in PISA do not show a relationship between the degree of competition and student performance […].
On the other hand, the results indicate a weak and negative relationship between the degree of competition and equity.
Among OECD countries, systems with more competition among schools tend to show a stronger impact of students' socio-economic status on their performance in mathematics. […T] his finding is consistent with research showing that school choice—and, by extension, school competition—is related to greater levels of segregation in the school system, which may have adverse consequences for equity in learning opportunities and outcomes. (pp. 53, 58)[6]

Summing up:

[A]fter socio-economic status is accounted for, private schools do not perform better than public schools; and schools that compete with other schools for students do not perform better than schools that don't compete. Thus, the cross-country analysis suggests that systems, as a whole, do not benefit from a greater prevalence of private schools or school competition. (p. 104)

Other telling findings, in this connection, are the following:

- *Selection and sorting of students*

Policies that regulate the selection and sorting of students into schools and classrooms can be related to performance in various ways. On the one hand, creating homogeneous student populations may allow teachers to direct classroom instruction to the specific needs of each group, maximizing the learning potential of each group. On the other hand, selecting and sorting students may end up segregating students according to socio-economic status and result in differences in learning opportunities. Grouping higher-achieving students together limits the opportunity for underachieving students to benefit by learning from their higher-achieving peers. In addition, if student sorting is related to teacher sorting, such that higher-achieving students are matched to the most talented teachers, underachieving students may be relegated to

---

[6] PISA is a triennial international comparative survey administered by OECD since 2000. While originally developed as an instrument for OECD countries, in PISA 2012 participated around 510,000 students representing about 28 million 15-year-olds in the schools of 65 countries (all 34 OECD member countries and 31 partner countries), representing more than 80 % of the world economy. As reads the Report of the PISA 2012 Results:

"What is important for citizens to know and be able to do?" That is the question that underlies the world's global metric for quality, equity and efficiency in school education known as the Programme for International Student Assessment (PISA). PISA assesses the extent to which 15-year-old students have acquired key knowledge and skills that are essential for full participation in modern societies. The assessment, which focuses on reading, mathematics, science and problem-solving, does not just ascertain whether students can reproduce what they have learned; it also examines how well they can extrapolate from what they have learned and apply that knowledge in unfamiliar settings, both in and outside of school. This approach reflects the fact that modern societies reward individuals not for what they know, but for what they can do with what they know. (www.oecd.org/pisa/keyfindings/pisa-2012-results-volume-I.pdf)

lower-quality instruction. Student selection and sorting may also create stereotypes and stigmas that could eventually affect student engagement and learning.
[...]
PISA 2012 results, like those of earlier PISA assessments, show that, in general, school systems that cater to different students' needs by separating students into different insti-tutions, grade levels and classes, known as stratification, have not succeeded in producing superior overall results, and in some cases, they have lower-than-average and more ineq-uitable performance. (pp. 76, 104)

- *Grade repetition*

  Grade repetition occurs when students, after a formal or informal assessment, are held back in the same grade for an additional year, rather than being promoted to the next stage along with their peers. This practice is usually perceived as an extra opportunity to fully acquire the required knowledge in order to move forward. However, research has consistently shown that grade repetition does not provide greater benefits than promotion to the next grade (Brophy 2006).
  [...]
  In addition to the financial costs, grade repetition widens inequities because the proportion of students from disadvantaged backgrounds who repeat a grade is higher than the pro-portion of advantaged students who repeat a grade. Students with low socio-economic status, low-educated parents or immigrant backgrounds, and boys are significantly more likely to repeat a grade than other students (OECD, 2011b). Grade repetition tends to widen the achievement gap between those who are held behind and their peers.
  [...]
  Indeed, students usually perceive repetition not as an enabling opportunity but as a personal punishment and social stigma and may be further discouraged from education. Grade repe-tition is a source of stress, ridicule and bullying by others, negatively affects self-esteem, and increases the likelihood of high-risk behaviours, school failure and dropout. (pp. 76, 78, 79)

- *Tracking students*

  The impact of the socio-economic status of students and/or schools on performance is stronger in school systems that sort students into different tracks, where students are grouped into different tracks at an early age, where more students attend vocational programmes, where more students attend academically selective schools, and where more students attend schools that transfer low-performing students or students with behaviour problems to another school. (p. 79)

- *School vouchers in Sweden*

  In the early 1990s, *Sweden* introduced major reforms to decentralize primary and secondary education to municipalities. In 1992, the government introduced a voucher programme enabling families to choose among public and private schools, known as independent schools.
  [...]
  Evidence of the impact on academic performance shows slight positive effects, although these are insignificant for students with low-educated parents or those from an immigrant background. The programme has also resulted in more segregation between schools (Nicaise et al., 2005). (p. 64)

- *Early childhood education*

  The benefits of investing in early childhood education and care are seen in the performance of 15-year-olds in PISA.
  Students who had attended pre-primary education for more than one year outperformed the rest; in many countries, the difference is equivalent to more than one school year, even

when taking into account the students' socio-economic background. There is, however, considerable cross-country variation on the impact, which may be explained by the quality of the education provided. Insufficient investment in early childhood education and care can lead to childcare shortages, low-quality education, unequal access and the segregation of children according to their family income—which, in turn, leads to inequities in schooling outcomes later (OECD, 2006). (p. 69)

In short, according to the Summary of 2012 PISA Results published by OECD[7]: "Although poor performance in school does not automatically stem from disadvantage, the socio-economic status of students and schools does appear to exert a powerful influence on learning outcomes" (p. 13). For example, "a more socio-economically advantaged student scores 39 points higher in mathematics—the equivalent of nearly one year of schooling—than a less-advantaged student". In addition, "students who reported that they had attended pre-primary school for more than one year score 53 points higher in mathematics—the equivalent of more than one year of schooling—than students who had not attended pre-primary education" (p. 12). Furthermore: "*Stratification* in school systems, which is the result of policies like grade repetition and selecting students at a young age for different 'tracks' or types of schools, is negatively related to equity; and students in highly stratified systems tend to be less motivated than those in less-stratified systems" (p. 24). In a letter addressed to the OECD General Secretary, commenting on the 2012 PISA results, the General Secretary of Education International (the largest international federation of professional organizations in the education field) concluded: "There is little difference between the performance of schools in the private sector and the public sector when the social background of students has been taken into account".[8]

As far as testing is concerned:

Critics argue that standardised tests may reinforce the advantages of schools that serve students from socio-economically advantaged backgrounds (Ladd and Walsh, 2002; Downey, Von Hippel and Hughes, 2008), or that teachers may respond to accountability measures by sorting out or retaining disadvantaged students (Jacob, 2005; Jennings, 2005). Standardised tests might have the adverse effect of limiting school goals to passing or proficiency on particular tests and focusing instruction on those students who are close to average proficiency and ignoring those who are far below or above the average (Neal and Schanzenback, 2010). (p. 67)

Besides dogmatically presuming the superiority of private over public schools, neoliberal education politics tends to dissolve the integrity of the school's mission and to disfigure the uniqueness and fullness of the teaching profession into the economic–professional dimension of education. *Standardized testing* is enthroned at the *school altar* as a *god* whose *priests* are teachers and whose *last judgment* sends some schools and teachers to heaven and the others to hell.

The biggest school-cheating scandal in the history of the USA, revealed in 2011, should be sufficient to make clear the potential of perversity and to discredit such policies. In the Atlanta school system, nearly 180 teachers have been implicated in

---

[7] www.oecd.org/pisa/keyfindings/pisa-2012-results-overview.pdf.

[8] http://download.ei-ie.org/Docs/WebDepot/Circular_PISA2012_E.pdf.

it and 35 teachers and administrators were indicted on charges of racketeering and corruption, in March 2013, among them the former Superintendent (Beverly Hall), once a national star for turning around test scores. For boosting standardized test scores, they fixed incorrect answers. According to the investigation Report,[9] the main causes of the scandal were the following:

- The targets set by the district were often unrealistic, especially given their cumulative effect over the years. Additionally, the administration put unreasonable pressure on teachers and principals to achieve targets;
- A culture of fear, intimidation and retaliation spread throughout the district; and
- Dr. Hall and her administration emphasized test results and public praise to the exclusion of integrity and ethics.

The neoliberal education politics has neither legitimacy, nor success, nor future. Referring to USA, Margaret LeCompte (2009) affirms: "It could be argued that destruction of the public school system was the intent of neoliberal educational reforms from the beginning" (p. 50). David Hursh (2007) concludes:

> Given what the aforementioned research tells us about the processes of schooling when systems of testing and accountability are created—the curriculum is narrowed and simplified, students who score low on tests are abandoned, poorly constructed tests lead to mass failures, and students are pushed out of schools—it should not be surprising that the achievement gap is growing larger rather than smaller. (p. 508)

In sum: "Market-driven educational reforms tend to deny that differences exist between corporations that process raw materials and institutions whose 'raw materials' are human" (Ichilov 2009, p. 43). As a consequence, "the meaning of education is controlled by the market, not by the democratic purposes of education, not by a child-centred approach, or by the right to education" (p. 37).

2.2 The Human Rights Approach to Education Quality Highlights the Normative Content of the Right to Education that Is not Whatever Right to Whatever Education, but the Right to an Education as a Fundamental Human Right and as a Global Public Good

As a UNESCO Report (UNESCO 2000) observed, at the end of the twentieth century:

> While it is apparent from the foregoing chapters that there has been a great deal of progress worldwide over the past half century towards implementation of the right to education in terms of access to education, it nevertheless remains that the vision that came to be embodied in Article 26 of the Universal Declaration of Human Rights was not just a quantitative one. It was also a qualitative one concerning the purposes and hence contents of education. (p. 74)

---

[9] http://ftpcontent.worldnow.com/wgcl/apsfindings/Volume%203%20of%203.pdf.

In this light, we can understand why the expression "everyone has the right to education" does not mean the same thing as to have "the right to an education" or "to be educated". The Convention on the Rights of the Child (United Nations, 1989)[10]—that is the most universal human rights treaty, being already in force in 194 countries—was a landmark for the mainstreaming of education quality required by the right to education. The Committee on the Rights of the Child stressed in its first General Comment (CRC/GC/2001/1),[11] referring to the Convention, that "article 29(1) underlines the individual and subjective right to a specific quality of education" (para. 9), which "reflects the rights and inherent dignity of the child" (para. 2).

The human rights approach to education quality reflects, therefore, human rights values and principles. It crosses the normative, programmatic and other texts adopted by the International Community since the beginning of the 1990s. "Quality education for all young people: Challenges, trends and priorities" was the theme of the 47th session of the International Conference on Education, held in Geneva in 2004.[12] *A human-rights-based approach to education for all—A framework for the realization of children's right to education and rights within education*—is the title of an edition prepared jointly by UNICEF (United Nations Children's Fund) and UNESCO, published in 2007. "It identifies *rights-holders* (and their entitlements) and corresponding *duty-bearers* (and their obligations) and works towards strengthening the capacities of rights-holders to make their claims, and of duty-bearers to meet their obligations" (UNICEF/UNESCO 2007, p. 116).

The human rights approach to education quality echoes, for instance, in the conclusions of the OECD Ministers of Education meeting, in Paris, on November 4–5, 2010 ("OECD Education Ministerial Meeting—Investing in Human and Social Capital: New Challenges"),[13] when they stated: "Education is a public good". It has not merely economic goals but aims at "equity" and "social cohesion" too. It contributes to "health, civic participation, political engagement, trust and tolerance". Moreover, "non-cognitive skills such as creativity, critical thinking, problem solving and team work are important for both economic and social

---

[10] www.ohchr.org/Documents/ProfessionalInterest/crc.pdf.

[11] www.unhchr.ch/tbs/doc.nsf/(symbol)/CRC.GC.2001.1.En?OpenDocument

Each State Party to the core human rights treaties is under an obligation to submit regular reports to Committees of experts that supervise how the rights are being implemented. The Committees are widely known as 'Treaty Bodies' or 'Treaty Monitoring Bodies'. General Comment or General Recommendation is a Committee's interpretation of the content of a treaty provisions, either related to a specific article or to a broader thematic issue. They often seek to clarify the reporting duties of States Parties and suggest approaches to implementing the human rights concerned.

[12] www.ibe.unesco.org/en/areas-of-action/international-conference-on-education-ice/47th-session-2004.html.

[13] www.oecd.org/dataoecd/53/16/46335575.pdf.

outcomes". A broad vision of quality education is proposed in the Council of Europe "Recommendation CM/Rec(2012)13 of the Committee of Ministers to member States on ensuring quality education"[14]:

> Considering that while access to education is in itself an important right, the true value of this right can only be realised if education is of adequate quality and if learning opportunities and arrangements enable pupils and students to complete their education in reasonable time and under conditions conducive to quality education. […]

> 6. For the purposes of this recommendation, 'quality education' is understood as education which:

> a. gives access to learning to all pupils and students, particularly those in vulnerable or disadvantaged groups, adapted to their needs as appropriate;
> b. provides a secure and non-violent learning environment in which the rights of all are respected;
> c. develops each pupil's and student's personality, talents and mental and physical abilities to their fullest potential and encourages them to complete the educational programmes in which they enrol;
> d. promotes democracy, respect for human rights and social justice in a learning environment which recognises everyone's learning and social needs;
> e. enables pupils and students to develop appropriate competences, self-confidence and critical thinking to help them become responsible citizens and improve their employability;
> f. passes on universal and local cultural values to pupils and students while equipping them also to make their own decisions;
> g. certifies outcomes of formal and non-formal learning in a transparent way based on fair assessment enabling acquired knowledge and competences to be recognized for further study, employment and other purposes;
> h. relies on qualified teachers who are committed to continuous professional development;
> i. is free of corruption.

The respective "Explanatory Memorandum" of the Steering Committee for Education Policy and Practice[15] comments:

> The recommendation is mainly concerned with defining the principles of public responsibility and recognises that various countries may choose to exercise this responsibility in different ways. It also recognises that public responsibility may be exercised directly by the competent public authority or authorities or by another body—public or private—mandated to exercise the responsibility on behalf of the competent authority. In the latter case, public responsibility is delegated but not abdicated: the competent public authority may withdraw the mandate of the body exercising public responsibility on its behalf and will have a duty to do so should the body to which responsibility is delegated exercise it irresponsibly or in other ways unsatisfactorily.

---

[14]   https://wcd.coe.int/ViewDoc.jsp?id=2014671andSite=CM.

[15]   https://wcd.coe.int/ViewDoc.jsp?Ref=CM(2012)121andLanguage=lanEnglishandVer=addfinal andSite=CMandBackColorInternet=DBDCF2andBackColorIntranet=FDC864andBackColorLogged =FDC864.

In light of the normative content of the right to education, as internationally agreed, quality education is therefore a complex concept, with material and non-material dimensions, such as:

- Material dimension: availability (both physically and economically), accessibility and equipment of safe, healthy and functional educational settings; financial and human means; teaching/learning resources; teachers' pay, etc.
- Non-material dimension: respect for the cultural, social and individual diversity of students; non-discrimination, inclusiveness and equity; school leadership and discipline; curricular relevance regarding the needs and interests of students, the characteristics of communities, the problems of societies and of Humankind; a good *ratio* of teacher/students; evaluation methods; teachers' personal qualities, motivation and competence, etc.
- Aesthetic dimension: the educational influence of the beauty of the material and immaterial forms mediating the right to education, including the education setting's architecture, as well as the educators' appearance, communication and personality.

Consequently, quality education results from the interaction between tangible and intangible ingredients, making it difficult to find stark measurable correlations. "Education remains very much a black box in which inputs are turned into outputs in ways that are difficult to predict or quantify consistently" (Pearson 2012, p. 7). Schools are complex and dynamic environments.

While there is no recipe or ready-to-wear approach to producing quality education, there are principles universally valid and applicable, forming a common pedagogic heritage of Humankind amply consecrated by the Ethics of the Right to Education. In addition, every country can learn from the most exemplar ones.

References

Hursh, D. (2007). Assessing no child left behind and the rise of neoliberal education policies. *American Educational Research Journal, 44*(3), 493–518.

Ichilov, O. (2009). *The retreat from public education: Global and Israeli perspectives*. Dordrecht: Springer Science+Business Media B.V.

Kant, I. (1803). *On education* ('Über Pädagogik', A. Churton, with an Introduction by C. A. Foley Rhys Davids, Trans.). Boston: D. C. Heath and Co. Publishers (1906). http://archive.org/details/kantoneducationu00kantuoft

LeCompte, M. (2009). Trends in research on teaching: An historical and critical overview. In L. Saha & A. Dworkin (Eds.), *International handbook of research on teachers and teaching* (pp. 25–60). New York: Springer Science+Business Media, LLC.

OECD. (1989). *Les écoles et la qualité—Un rapport international*. Paris: OECD Publishing.

OECD. (2014). *Equity, excellence and inclusiveness in education: Policy lessons from around the world*. Paris: OECD Publishing (by Andreas Schleicher). Retrieved June 2014, from http://teachfirstnz.org/images/uploads/Documents/OECD.pdf

Pearson. (2012). *Lessons in country performance in education—2012 report*. London: The Learning Curve, Economist Intelligence Unit. http://thelearningcurve.pearson.com/the-report

Spring, J. (2000). *The universal right to education: Justification, definition, and guidelines.* London: Lawrence Erlbaum Associates Publishers.

Supiot, A. (2005). *Homo juridicus—Essai sur la fonction anthropologique du Droit.* Paris: Éditions du Seuil, Points-Essai.

UNESCO. (2000). *World education report—2000—The right to education: towards education for all throughout life.* New York: UNESCO Publishing. www.unesco.org/education/information/wer/PDFeng/wholewer.PDF

UNICEF/UNESCO. (2007). *A human rights-based approach to education for all: A framework for the realization of children's right to education and rights within education.* www.unicef.org/publications/files/A_Human_Rights_Based_Approach_to_Education_for_All.pdf

Védrine, H. (2007). *Rapport pour le Président de la République sur la France et la Mondialisation.* Retrieved July 2014, from http://medias.lemonde.fr/mmpub/edt/doc/20070905/951341_rapport_d-hubert_vedrine.pdf

Chapter 3
Most Far-Reaching Lessons from Studies, Reforms and Reports Concerning Education Systems and the Teaching Profession Worldwide

Abstract The human species being essentially perfectible and educable, the primacy of education is a recurrent theme in the classic sources of pedagogic thought. It has been endowed with the status of a human right, and *key* is a word often used to indicate the paramountcy of the right to education. Nevertheless, while it is largely recognized that education is the great "social equalizer" and that achieving both educational "excellence" and "equity" is one of the most critical problems of our times, education systems are not keeping up with increasingly multicultural and rapidly changing societies. They need radical reforms. A reform is not radical enough if it does not grasp the roots of what is failing. In addition, it must be systemic and holistic, taking into account the interaction of education with the whole society since human rights are essentially indivisible and interdependent. Although teachers are the real genius of the everyday alchemy of education quality, two terms are frequently used with respect to the status of the teaching profession worldwide: "decline" and (lack of) "recognition". The minimum that may be said is that it is uncared for: it is uncared for when Governments do not care for it and it does not care for itself. The quality of the teaching profession is neither cheap nor evaluable in snapshot, but what is at stake in education is priceless. Finland's education system is example of a human rights approach to education quality, driven by a highly qualified and ranked teaching profession. It epitomizes the compatibility between equity and quality, inclusiveness and competitiveness, thus making more evident, by contrast, how miserable neoliberal education politics is.

Keywords Primacy of education · Education systems · Teaching profession · Reforms · Finland

There are significant lines of international convergence and consensus.

Comparisons between countries are valuable for a number of reasons. First, they broaden the view of what is possible. Too often, policymakers remain stuck with conventional ideas, bound by precedents in their own context, and are unable to see options that might be available and successful. By providing policymakers with an expanded view of the policy choices that might be available, comparisons can expand the toolbox. Second, international comparisons show how ideas work in practice at the system level. By exploring other

© The Author(s) 2015   19
A. Reis Monteiro, *The Teaching Profession*, SpringerBriefs in Education,
DOI 10.1007/978-3-319-12130-7_3

systems in depth, policymakers can see what the implementation challenges are, how other nations dealt with them, and what remains to be solved. Such explorations can help enable policymakers put in place new policies with a clearer eye. (Darling-Hammond and Rothman 2011, p. 1)

The Report of *The 2011 International Summit on the Teaching Profession* reads too:

Summit participants agreed that there was enormous value in learning from international comparisons on this subject. Such comparisons help us get outside our own contexts and established patterns of thinking; show where some of the successes and failures have been; and broaden our views of possible options and trade-offs. They help us to think anew, to encourage innovation, and to design new approaches informed by the world's best practices. (Asia Society 2011, p. 26)

The following highlights the main findings arising from the aforementioned international and national reports and studies.

3.1 Education Drives Individual, Social as Well as Universal Destinies, but the School Is not up to Its Contemporary Mission

The human species being essentially perfectible and educable, the primacy of education is a recurrent theme in the classic sources of pedagogic thought. Education has often been considered guilty of the evils of societies and also, paradoxically, prized as the main resource to correct them as well. As Kant (1803) taught, "with education is involved the great secret of the perfection of human nature" (p. 7).

The primacy of education was often evoked during the *travaux préparatoires* (elaboration) of the main international standards of International Human Rights Law, which recognize the relative priority of the right to education. Such a priority has been rediscovered by the International Community during the last decade of the twentieth century, and the right to education has been put on the International Agenda, as numerous high-level conferences, declarations, programs of action and other initiatives testify.

In reality, without overlooking the principle of the indivisibility and interdependence of all human rights, three human rights appear as having real priority, in deep dialectical interaction: the right to life, the right to education and the right to development. The right to education may be considered as the most fundamental for a *human* life, that is a life with dignity, liberty, equality, creativity and responsibility. It is largely recognized as the very engine of development in its individual and collective—e.g. cultural, political, economic and ecological—dimensions. It is the most powerful resource for the survival and perfecting of the human species.

Therefore, *key* is a word often used in the texts of the United Nations' bodies and high representatives to indicate the paramountcy of the right to education. For instance, the Special Rapporteur on the Right to Education (Katarina Tomaševski) stressed in one of her annual reports: "Education is increasingly defined as the key to development and the right to education as the key to the enjoyment of many other human rights" (E/CN.4/2001/52, para. 79).[1] In another Report, she observed that consequences of denying the right to education "cannot be retroactively remedied" (E/CN.4/2004/45, para. 8).[2]

Education is, therefore, no more envisaged as only a domestic familial, political and instrumental matter, but also as an international and ethical issue. If the link between education, economy and work has been the most socially and individually important (and remains the most visible), the right to education is principally a source of human worth and dignity, cultural and individual identity, and enlightened and active citizenship, without forgetting its power for social mobility and equalization. "From the human rights viewpoint, education is thus an end in itself rather than merely a means for achieving other ends", as Tomaševski underlined (E/CN.4/1999/49, para. 13).[3]

As a consequence: "Success requires a clear vision and belief in the centrality of education for students and the nation" (OECD 2011b, p. 173) that should be "a long-term vision and a shared dream" (Asia Society 2012, p. 24), and a school up to its human and civilizational mission.

Notwithstanding, as notes the Report of the New York 2011 Summit on the Teaching Profession: "At a time when the society had changed, the economy had changed, and the understanding of learning had changed, only schools had remained static" (Asia Society 2011, p. 9).[4] The Report of the New York 2012 Summit reads too: "Throughout the Summit was a palpable sense of urgency that the aims and processes of schooling in the twenty-first century need to be fundamentally different from those in the twentieth century". In effect: "In the twentieth century, education centered on teaching a relatively fixed core of content. This 'knowledge transmission' model of education is no longer adequate" (Asia Society 2012, p. 6). Paraphrasing what was said by a participant in the Summit, the school of the twenty-first century should not keep functioning following the logic of the nineteenth century and with teachers keeping in the twentieth.

> A major tension in education systems today, in fact, is the distance between the rhetoric of twenty-first century skills and the reality of schooling. In particular, as a representative of Norway pointed out, we say we value twenty-first century skills but only test basic skills. Some countries say that they want to develop creative, confident students who are adept in a range of areas, but they only test basic reading and math skills. […]
> Bold steps will be needed to close the gap between what we measure and what we value or we risk driving education systems in the wrong direction. (pp. 9, 23)

---

[1] www.unhchr.ch/Huridocda/Huridoca.nsf/0/8774217173a3fde0c1256a10002ecb42/$FILE/G0110177.pdf.

[2] www.unhchr.ch/Huridocda/Huridoca.nsf/e06a5300f90fa0238025668700518ca4/05af86414ce9 03c9c1256e3000357284/$FILE/G0410332.pdf.

[3] www.unhchr.ch/Huridocda/Huridoca.nsf/TestFrame/6a76ced2c8c9efc780256738003abbc8? Opendocument.

[4] This Summit "was the first to bring together ministers of education and teachers' union leaders from many countries to the same table" (p. 3). A second took place in New York in 2012; the third met in Amsterdam in 2013; the fourth in Wellington, New Zealand, in 2014; the fifth is scheduled to take place in Banff, Alberta (Canada), in 2015.

In effect, as "public examinations are the baton that conducts the entire orchestra […] unless these change, nothing else will change" (Barber et al. 2012, p. 58).

In short, while it is largely recognized that education is the great "social equalizer" and that achieving both educational "excellence" and "equity" is one of the most critical problems of our times, education systems are not keeping up with increasingly multicultural and rapidly changing societies. School does not do all that it should do, and often does badly most of what it does.

3.2 Education Systems Need Radical and Holistic Reforms Addressing Both Their Tangible and Intangible Dimensions

The McKinsey and Company Report *How the World's Best-performing School Systems come out on Top*[5] remarks: "Education reform is top of the agenda of almost every country in the world", but "the performance of many school systems has barely improved in decades" (Barber and Mourshed 2007, Executive Summary). For instance, in England, "a report published by the National Foundation for Education Research in 1996 demonstrated that between 1948 and 1996, despite 50 years of reform, there had been no measurable improvement in standards of literacy and numeracy in English schools" (p. 10).

Regarding the teaching profession, a French Report notices that much of its findings on the status of the teaching profession in France are the same as those already found by other past Commissions, since the Commission chaired by Alexandre Ribot (1899), through the Louis Joxe Commission (1972), until the Claude Thélot Commission (2004): bureaucracy, Taylorism, uniformity, lack of spaces and other working conditions, *malaise* [uneasiness], etc. (Pochard 2008, pp. 12, 13, 52).

Referring to the USA, LeCompte (2009) wrote: "One of the principal problems facing United States' education in the early 2000s is that a complete mismatch exists between the diagnosis of educational problems and the remedies proposed" (p. 45). That is why an American study concluded: "The one thing that is indispensable is a new system" (National Center on Education and the Economy 2007, p. 9). Indeed, the education systems worldwide, in general, are still waiting for the radical reform needed to break the vicious circle of their deadlocks. In this respect, an OECD Report (2011b) points out:

---

[5] This Report accounts for research carried out in 25 school systems in Asia, Europe, North America and the Middle East, between May 2006 and March 2007. The schools visited were selected to represent the world's top ten best-performing school systems, according to the results of the PISA (Program for International Student Assessment), launched in 1997 by OECD to assess the educational systems, but it also included others that are improving rapidly, some of them in developing countries (Bahrain, Brazil, Qatar, Saudi Arabia, and the United Arab Emirates), which are adopting successful approaches.

['R]eform' is not equivalent to improvement. 'Improvement' means doing what the system has been doing all along, but more and better. 'Reform' involves paradigm shifts. In other words, the notion of a *reform* entails an awareness that further development of education is not only a matter of remedying perceived shortcomings; it is an understanding that more fundamental issues exist where education has to catch up with changes in society. Without such an understanding, any 'improvement' of the system and practices only reinforces what might have gone wrong. (p. 106)

A reform is not radical enough if it does not grasp the roots of what is failing. In addition, it must be systemic and holistic, taking into account the interaction of education with the whole society. Human rights are indivisible and interdependent. "Bring on the whole-system revolution!" (Barber et al. 2012, p. 64).

The variables of education systems' success include the education budget and decentralization. As far as budget is concerned: "OECD analyses show that the level of financial expenditures in a system is not closely related to its quality or equity. It is how the resources are used to address key challenges that make a difference" (Asia Society 2014, p. 5). In effect:

[A]fter a certain threshold of expenditure, the way resources are spent is more important than the total amount spent. […] Excellence and equity in student performance are less related to a country's income or expenditure on education than to how those educational resources are allocated, and to the policies, practices and learning environments that determine the conditions in which students work. (OECD 2014, pp. 27, 101)

Decentralization may occur in a variety of ways: delegation of authority for curriculum and assessment, and/or for resources and personnel as well, and/or increasing innovation and competition among schools for increasing parents' choice. Another OECD Report (2011b) notes: "Decentralisation is the overwhelming focus for the current literature on education planning and governance, but the subject may deserve a more nuanced look" (p. 107).

PISA shows that school systems that grant more autonomy to schools to define and elaborate their curricula and assessments tend to perform better than systems that don't grant such autonomy […]. In contrast, greater responsibility in managing resources appears to be unrelated to a school system's overall performance (OECD 2013a, Table IV.1.4).
The positive relationship between schools' autonomy in defining and elaborating curricula and assessment policies and student performance that is observed at the level of the school system can play out differently within countries. […] The degree of school autonomy is also related to the socio-economic status and demographic background of students and schools and various other school characteristics, such as whether the school is public or private. […]
The relationship between school autonomy and performance also appears to be affected by whether there is a culture of collaboration between teachers and principals in managing a school. (OECD 2014, pp. 48, 52)

In addition: "Giving teachers more autonomy can be counterproductive if the quality and education of the teachers are inadequate" (p. 6).

Decentralization and schools' autonomy are, therefore, a double-edged sword. A balance between central and local responsibilities is most likely to suit the requirements for the right to education.

Last but not least, the education system interacts with other social systems. As an OECD Report (2014) reads:

> Across OECD countries, almost one in five students does not reach a basic minimum level of skills to function in society, and roughly the same proportion of students drops out of school before completing their secondary education.
> [...]
> In terms of fairness, PISA shows that socio-economic disadvantage is closely related to many of the student and school characteristics that are associated with performance. Although poor performance in school does not automatically stem from disadvantage, the socio-economic status of students and schools does appear to exert a powerful influence on learning outcomes [...]. Because advantaged families are better able to reinforce and enhance the effects of schools, because students from advantaged families may attend higher-quality schools, or because schools are simply better-equipped to nurture and develop young people from advantaged backgrounds, in many countries, schools tend to reproduce existing patterns of socio-economic advantage, rather than create a more equitable distribution of learning opportunities and outcomes. (pp. 12, 19)

According to the same report:

> Investing in equity in education and in reducing dropout pays off. [...] While such estimates are never wholly certain, they do suggest that the benefits of improving individuals' cognitive skills dwarf any conceivable cost of improvement.
> Improving students' performance in school can also encourage healthier lifestyles and participation in democratic institutions and other civil society initiatives and organisations – all of which reduces the cost to society. The Survey of Adult Skills, conducted by the OECD in 2012, shows that skills are positively associated with self-reported good health, political interest and interpersonal trust (OECD 2013a). Crime and other illegal activities may decrease, since better-educated people tend to be less involved in criminality (OECD 2010b). Indeed many economic and social problems, such as teenage pregnancy and unhealthy habits, are linked to low levels of educational attainment and skills (Cunha and Heckman 2007; Heckman 2008).
> Strengthening equity in education, and investing in the early years, also yield high returns. Starting strong in education makes it easier to acquire skills and knowledge later on. For children from disadvantaged backgrounds, access to early education not only contributes to equity, but is, in the long run, economically efficient as well. (p. 19)

In short: "To succeed, reform efforts cannot tackle just one small piece of the puzzle but must instead be part of a comprehensive approach" (Asia Society 2011, p. 26). Otherwise, "the system wins every time".

> What these findings tell policy makers is that while there are several features that are shared among high-performing systems, among systems with greater equity, or among high-performing schools, no one policy or practice spells success.
> What is important is a cohesive and systematic approach, as education policies and practices, resources invested in education, the learning environment, socio-economic status, demographics and education outcomes are all interrelated. (OECD 2014, p. 105)

In any case, another "broad conclusion is that of those variables which are potentially open to policy influence, factors to do with teachers and teaching are the most important influences on student learning. In particular, the broad consensus is that 'teacher quality' is the single most important school variable influencing student achievement" (OECD 2005, pp. 26, 27).

3.3   Teachers Are the Genius of the Everyday Alchemy of Education Quality, but the Teaching Profession Is Declining

Following the McKinsey and Company Report: "The quality of an education system cannot exceed the quality of its teachers" (Barber and Mourshed 2007, p. 40). The 2010 OECD Ministers of Education meeting aforementioned[6] concluded: "Teachers are the key [… but] respect for the profession may be falling". Because of that: "We saw the need to raise the status and esteem of teachers".

Two terms are frequently used with respect to the status of the teaching profession worldwide: *decline* and (lack of) *recognition*. For example:

- A report of the Parliament of the Commonwealth of Australia (1998) affirmed: "The status of teachers in Australia is declining. This was the view expressed almost universally to the Committee by teachers, students, academics, professional associations, parent organisations and bureaucrats. It is a view supported by the general literature on the subject and by specific research findings" (p. 29). According to the OECD (2005) study: "There are a number of countries where teaching is held in high regard as a career", but it is widespread "the view that teaching is a profession in long-term decline" (p. 39).[7] Following Christine Blower, General Secretary of the National Union of Teachers (NUT), in England and Wales:

  Morale in the teaching profession is at dangerously low levels. This is reflected starkly in the results of an NUT-commissioned YouGov survey that was published at the turn of 2013. This saw more than half (55 %) of teachers describe their morale as low or very low, an increase of 13 % since teachers were asked the same question in April 2012. The later survey also found 69 % of teachers reporting a decline in their morale since the last general election. (in Leslie 2013, p. 70)

- If the decline of the teaching profession is not steady in every country, more widespread is the feeling of lack of recognition of its professionals. According to John MacBeath (2012): "Wherever teachers have been questioned about their priorities and satisfiers, in South America, Sub-Saharan Africa, Europe or North America, they cite the importance of recognition and respect for the challenges they rise to on a daily basis" (p. 12). The abovementioned French Report remarks: "Teachers met by the Commission spontaneously express a demand for recognition more than ambitions concerning career" (Pochard 2008, p. 166).

The minimum that may be said is that the teaching profession is uncared for: it is uncared for when Governments do not care for it, and it does not care for itself.

---

[6]   www.oecd.org/dataoecd/53/16/46335575.pdf.

[7]   This OECD study, titled *Teachers matter: Attracting, developing and retaining effective teachers*, accounts for the results of a major survey conducted by its Directorate for Education, over the years 2002–2004, in collaboration with 25 countries in all continents but Africa. It is about the recruitment, preparation, career and working conditions of school teachers.

- Governments do not care for the teaching profession when the neoliberal managerial ideology prevails, according to which to be professional is to perform whatever commands zealously and proudly, as mere "deliverers of the curriculum" (OECD 2011a, p. 5). In the USA, for example, "teachers have tended to accept the intensification of their work" as a signal of their increasing professionalism, which may be used ideologically to legitimate just its contrary (Ginsburg and Megahed 2009, p. 542). It amounts to a deprofessionalization of the teaching profession, which is treated as a "craft", providing for its further control and instrumentalization. As Dean Holmes said to his students in Harvard in 1930, a nation whose teachers "perform, in general, little and mechanic tasks, strictly controlled, coming directly from manuals and following strictly instructions, is close to put its future under the rule of second class spirits" (cit. in Bourdoncle 1993, p. 113).
- The profession does not care for itself when teachers are not the best advocates of their cause if they neglect, as a Report of the Joint ILO/UNESCO Committee of Experts on the Application of the Recommendation concerning the Status of Teachers (UNESCO 1966)[8] reads, "to promote their own status and professionalism", thus allowing "a community perception to develop that their main preoccupation has been with their own salaries and benefits". When teachers are mainly concerned with their economic–labour interests, and not enough with the values, dignity and prestige of the profession, their professional conscience, attitudes and conduct are likely to fail. A symptom of that is the broad lack of awareness of the importance of Professional Ethics in education, as well as teachers' lack of appetite for a self-governing body.

Lawrence Saha and Anthony Dworkin (2009) concluded: "The conditions of teachers and teaching have become common across national boundaries so that uniformity rather than diversity dominates the practices" (p. 10). In fact, as Lorin Anderson (2004) observed: "Even in industrialized nations, deteriorating working conditions and low salaries are discouraging people from entering the teaching profession" (p. 19). The overall status of the teaching profession is summarized in Sect. 2.2.1.

Some colours of this portrait are reflected in the first paragraph of the Executive Summary of a fresh OECD survey—*TALIS 2013 Results*[9]:

---

[8] www.ilo.org/wcmsp5/groups/public/—ed_dialogue/—sector/documents/meetingdocument/wcms_162259.pdf.

[9] www.oecd.org/edu/school/TALIS-2013-Executive-Summary.pdf
TALIS is so described in *A Teachers' Guide to TALIS 2013*:

The OECD Teaching and Learning International Survey (TALIS) is a large scale international survey that focuses on the working conditions of teachers and the learning environment in schools. TALIS, a collaboration among participating countries and economies, the OECD, an international research consortium, social partners and the European Commission, aims to provide valid, timely and comparable information to help countries review and define policies for developing a high-quality teaching workforce.TALIS examines the ways in which teachers' work is recognized, appraised and rewarded, and assesses teachers' participation in professional development activities. The study provides insights into

Our view of teachers is coloured by our own experience as students. This firsthand – and often dated – knowledge is augmented by the portrayal of teachers and their working conditions in the media. Thus, in many countries, the traditional view of teaching is one in which teachers work alone in classrooms, behind closed doors, often with larger numbers of students than they can realistically handle. In some countries, teaching is seen as a job without real career prospects that young people enter if they cannot get into a better one. The fact that pay tends to be lower than that of other college graduates is compensated for by the fact that teachers often enjoy more holiday time and are seen as working fewer hours than their colleagues in other fields.

The same survey includes the following findings:

- While more than nine out of ten (91 %) teachers are satisfied with their jobs and nearly eight in ten (78 %) would choose the teaching profession again, less than one in three teachers believe teaching is a valued profession in society.
- Sixty-eight percentage of teachers are women, except in Japan, and the average age is 43, with Singapore having the youngest teachers and Italy the oldest.
- The average class size is 24 students, and of an average total of 38 h of work, per week, teachers spend an average of:

  - Nineteen-hour teaching, ranging from 15 h in Norway to 27 h in Chile;
  - Seven hours in preparing lessons;
  - Five hours marking/grading;
  - Two hours on school management, working with parents and extracurricular activities.

- In about half the countries, one in four teachers said they spend at least 30 % of class time handling classroom disruptions and administrative tasks.
- The areas where most teachers said they needed more training are teaching students with special needs (22 %), followed by information and communication technology skills (19 %).
- According to most teachers, formal appraisals have little impact on career advancement or financial recognition, around half of them reporting feeling that most appraisals are carried out merely as administrative task.

(Footnote 9 continued)

teachers' beliefs about and attitudes towards teaching, the pedagogical practices that they adopt, and the factors related to teachers' sense of self-efficacy and job satisfaction. TALIS also examines the roles of school leaders and the support they give their teachers.

The first cycle of TALIS was conducted in 2008 and surveyed teachers and school leaders of lower secondary education in 24 countries. In 2013, 34 countries and economies participated in TALIS. (www.oecd.org/edu/school/TALIS-Teachers-Guide.pdf)

More than 100,000 teachers and school leaders at lower secondary level (for students aged 11–16) took part in the OECD survey, but it should be noted that TALIS cannot be seen as a "global 'selfie' by teachers", to the extent that from Central & South America only Mexico, Chile and Brazil participated, and none country from Africa.

3.4 Selecting, Educating and Evaluating Teachers in Light of Their Responsibilities, and Treating and Trusting Them as Professionals, Is Crucial to Quality Education

The first and broadly shared conclusion of the 2014 International Summit on the Teaching Profession was: "It is impossible to overestimate the importance of high-quality teachers to excellence and equity. Previous Summits had illustrated that the highest performing systems take a comprehensive approach to attracting, training, and retaining talented people in the profession" (Asia Society 2014, p. 27).

Regarding selection, an OECD Report (2014) observes:

> Successful enterprises often report that personnel selection is the most important set of decisions that they make. In the case of teaching, the evidence suggests that all too often the selection process follows rules about qualifications and seniority that bear little relationship to the qualities needed to be an effective teacher. (p. 37)

Furthermore, too many teachers are poorly prepared. An OECD Report published in (1990) noted "the mediocrity of pedagogic education" (p. 89). More than two decades later, an European Commission *Document* (2012) reads: "Teacher surveys regularly highlight the fact that many of them feel ill-equipped to deal with 'teaching special learning needs students', 'student discipline and behaviour' and 'ICT teaching skills'" (p. 35). MacBeath (2012) also concluded that "a common finding internationally is that teachers are generally unprepared for surviving and thriving in the world of classrooms" (p. 17).

While teacher educators are crucial for the quality of the teaching profession, "there is surprisingly little knowledge of how teacher educators are, themselves, prepared. In many OECD countries, universities enjoy complete autonomy in developing teacher education programmes, from curriculum to practicum requirements and professional qualification standards" (OECD 2014, p. 42). However, "most countries have no professional standards or models of competences for teacher educators (beyond the academic competences required of all Higher Education staff)" (European Commission 2012, p. 55).

In the New York 2011 Summit: "The area of sharpest discussion and disagreement was certainly the design and implementation of fair and effective teacher-evaluation systems" (Asia Society 2011, p. 26).

> There are also areas of emphatic disagreement, including the weight given to student test scores or value-added measures in teacher appraisals and the relationship of performance to rewards, especially bonuses or merit pay (as opposed to salary differentials that go with different career roles). It is also difficult to balance the goals of improvement and accountability. Poorly designed or top-down appraisal systems can unintentionally create a climate of fear and resistance among teachers that inhibits creativity. (Asia Society 2014, p. 10)

Reducing teachers' performance evaluation to instrumental, isolated elements—which are easier to observe, for the sake of objectifying and quantifying for statistical and bureaucratic purposes—is to avoid its complexity and holistic nature and, consequently, to disfigure it. The frenzy of data-driven accountability reaches a climax when teachers' test-based evaluations are published, naming and ranking individual teachers as effective or ineffective.[10]

According to an OECD Report (2011a), "giving teachers responsibility as professionals and leaders of reform", and trusting their professional responsibility, is "[p]erhaps the greatest challenge to reform" (pp. 5, 55).

The New York 2011 Summit Report affirms: "For the teaching profession to improve, teachers need to see themselves as autonomous professionals rather than just the subjects of management" (Asia Society 2011, p. 16). The New York 2012 Summit Report notes, referring to the USA: "Fundamentally, American society's view of teaching has to change from the factory model of yesterday to a view of teaching as a true profession" (Asia Society 2012, p. 9). Following the European Commission *Document* (2012):

> Recruiting excellent people into teaching requires a more attractive work environment – where teaching staff are treated like professionals, and have sufficient scope to work autonomously. According to recent reviews of the evidence, developing and retaining a motivated, committed teaching profession requires limiting 'dissatisfiers' and increasing 'satisfiers'. 'Dissatisfiers' for teaching staff include: feeling not in control, lack of time for all work required, isolation from colleagues; prescribed curricula, bureaucracy, pressure to meet targets, testing, an overload of new policies and initiatives; lack of parental support, poor student behaviour and stress. The 'satisfiers' concern: being valued, trusted and listened to; adequate time for learning, teaching and planning; autonomy, initiative, creativity; contact with pupils, collegiality; scope for innovation and experimentation. (p. 31)

The *A Teachers' Guide to TALIS 2013*[11] reaffirms: "As for most professionals, teachers derive the most satisfaction from their work when they feel that they are treated as professionals, when their opinions are sought and valued, and when they feel they have a say in how they work" (p. 27).[12]

In sum, the teaching profession quality is neither cheap nor evaluable in snapshot, but what is at stake in education is priceless.

---

[10] This was done in the USA, in the State of New York, in 2012, where a teacher recognized as teacher of the year by the Parent Teacher Organization earned a score of 7 out of 20 points. Her school Principal wrote: "Despite the judgment of the New York State Education Department, Ashley remains a model teacher in our school: beloved by students and parents, respected by colleagues and supervisors" (Valerie Strauss, "Meet Ashley, a great teacher with a bad 'value-added' score". (Retrieved April 2013 from www.washingtonpost.com/blogs/answer-sheet/post/meet-ashley-a-great-teacher-with-a-bad-value-added-score/2012/09/13/27836e4e-fdb7-11e1-a31e-804fccb658f9_blog.html).

[11] www.oecd.org/edu/school/TALIS-Teachers-Guide.pdf.

[12] In this connection, an OECD Report (2011a) remarks:

> Unions are sometimes perceived as interfering with promising school reform programs by giving higher priority to the unions' 'bread and butter' issues than to what the evidence suggests students need to succeed. But the fact is that many of the countries with the strongest student performance also have strong teachers' unions, and the better a country's education system performs, the more likely that country is working constructively with its unions and treating its teachers as trusted professional partners. (p. 56).

3.5 Finland: An Admirable Public Education System with Human Right and Global Public Good Quality, as Well as a Very Prestigious and Esteemed Teaching Profession

• Beyond PISA

In 2001, when it appeared at the top of the ranking of the education systems assessed by PISA, Finland became a destiny of educational pilgrimage.[13] Finnish students had not been specifically taught to get such results. Thereafter, other countries began to "work for PISA" and got to the top, but by ways less admirable, even "unpalatable" (OECD 2011b, p. 152). In this respect, Pasi Sahlberg, the most mediatic ambassador of Finland's worldwide prized education system,[14] comments:

> One may also conclude that these international standardized tests are becoming global curriculum standards. Indeed, OECD has observed that its PISA test is already playing an important role in national policy making and education reforms in many countries. Schools, teachers and students are now prepared in advance to take these tests. Learning materials are adjusted to fit to the style of these assessments. Life in many schools around the world is becoming split into important academic study that these tests measure, and other not-so-important study that these measurements don't cover. Kind of a GERM in grand scale.[15]

---

[13] "Finnish schools have become a kind of tourist destination, with hundreds of educators and policy makers annually travelling to Helsinki to try to learn the secret of their success" (OECD 2011b, p. 118).

[14] 'How GERM is infecting schools around the world?', published in *The Washington Post* on 29 June 2012 (www.pasisahlberg.com/blog).

Pasi Sahlberg is the author of *Finnish Lessons: What can the world learn from educational change in Finland* (Teachers College Press 2011) that has earned him the 2013 University of Louisville Grawemeyer Award in Education (USA). He also received the 2012 Education Award of the Trade Union of Education in Finland. He wrote:

> Since the beginning of 2000, I have given more than 250 keynote addresses and 50 interviews about the Finnish educational system around the world. My estimate is that this means talking to some 50,000 people directly and many more through published stories and news. Numerous conversations with people who are interested in education like I am have greatly advanced writing this book. Following are some of the questions that have been asked over and over again: "What is the secret of Finnish educational success?", "How do you get best young people into teaching in Finland?", "How much does lack of ethnic diversity have to do with good educational performance there?", "How do you know that all schools are doing what they should when you don't test students or inspect teachers?", and "How did Finland save its education system during the economic downturn in the 1990s?" (Sahlberg 2011, p. 2).

[15] http://dianeravitch.net/2012/12/14/exclusive-pasi-sahlberg-on-timss-and-pirls.

What is GERM?

Ten years ago – against all odds – Finland was ranked as the world's top education nation. It was strange because in Finland education is seen as a public good accessible to all free of charge without standardized testing or competitive private schools. When I look around the world, I see competition, choice, and measuring of students and teachers as the main means to improve education. This market-based global movement has put many public schools at risk in the United States and many other countries, as well. But not in Finland. […]
One thing that has struck me is how similar education systems are. […]
Education reforms in different countries also follow similar patterns. So visible is this common way of improvement that I call it the Global Educational Reform Movement or GERM. It is like an epidemic that spreads and infects education systems through a virus. […] Education systems borrow policies from others and get infected. As a consequence, schools get ill, teachers don't feel well, and kids learn less. GERM infections have various symptoms. The first symptom is more competition within education systems. […]
The second symptom of GERM is increased school choice. It essentially positions parents as consumers empowering them to select schools for their children from several options and thereby promotes market-style competition into the system as schools seek to attract those parents. […] Increasing numbers of charter schools in the United States, secondary school academies in England, free schools in Sweden and private schools in Australia are examples of expanding school choice policies. Yet according to the OECD, nations pursuing such choice have seen both a decline in academic results and an increase in school segregation. The third sign of GERM is stronger accountability from schools and related standardized testing of students. Just as in the market place, many believe that holding teachers and schools accountable for students' learning will lead to improved results. Today standardized test scores are the most common way of deciding whether schools are doing a good job. Teacher effectiveness that is measured using standardized tests is a related symptom of GERM. According to the Center for Public Education [USA], standardized testing has increased teaching to the test, narrowed curricula to prioritize reading and mathematics, and distanced teaching from the art of pedagogy to mechanistic instruction. […]
We should instead restore the fundamental meaning and values of school education. Without public schools, our nations and communities are poorly equipped to value humanity, equality and democracy. […] Diversity is richness in humanity and a condition for innovation.[16]

That is why Finnish teachers were neither very surprised nor excited with the news. "Many teachers and principals in Finland have a skeptical view of international measurements and benchmarking tools. They perceive teaching and learning as complex processes and are aware that quantifying their effectiveness is difficult" (Sahlberg 2011, p. 134). In addition, the PISA results are not *scholarly pure*, as already documented. According to the 2005 OECD study: "The first and most solidly based finding is that the largest source of variation in student learning is attributable to differences in what students bring to school—their abilities and attitudes, and family and community background" (p. 26).

Learning is not separate from learners' personal lives, socio-economic situation, or the attitudes, values, traditions, and beliefs held by their community. Making education systems more relevant and effective requires an approach that recognises the interconnecting

---

[16] "How GERM is infecting schools around the world?", published in *The Washington Post* on 29 June 2012 (www.pasisahlberg.com/blog).

roles played by many different stakeholders, including parents, wider society and government. (European Commission 2012, p. 20)

The value of the Finnish public education overcomes all that such international surveys are able to assess.

One point of view is that academic achievement tests, such as the Programme for International Student Assessment (PISA), Trends in International Mathematics and Science Study (TIMSS), and Progress in International Reading Literacy Study (PIRLS) focus on areas too narrow to capture the whole spectrum of school education, and thus ignore social skills, moral development, creativity, or digital literacy as important outcomes of public education for all […]. (Sahlberg 2011, p. 9)

Below are very briefly highlighted the main features of the Finnish education system.

• **Education System of Finland**

The Finnish education system is governed by the Ministry of Education (that has two Ministers: the Minister of Education and the Minister of Culture) and the National Board of Education (responsible for primary and secondary education as well as for adult education and training). It is composed of the following:

- Pre-primary education offered by day care centres, as well as in primary schools in the year preceding the beginning of basic education, at six years. It is voluntary, but is attended by some 96 % of the age group.
- Basic education in comprehensive schools (*peruskoulu*) begins at the age of seven and lasts 9 years. While it is provided within a single structure, without division into primary and lower secondary education, year classes 1–6 are mainly taught by class teachers and year classes 7–9 by specialized subject teachers.[17] It is completed by nearly all children (99.7 %).
- After basic education, a year of additional voluntary basic education is available that is attended by around 2.5 % students.
- Post-compulsory school education is designed to last 3 years, but may be completed from 2 to 4 years. It includes general and vocational upper secondary education and has a modular structure, i.e. not tied to year classes. It is attended by about 93 % of each age group (general: around 54.5 %; vocational: around 38.5 %) immediately after leaving comprehensive school. The certification is delivered when the required number of courses is complete.
- General upper secondary schooling ends with a national Matriculation Examination that includes a test in the mother tongue and in three of the following subjects: the second national language (Swedisch or Sami), a foreign language, mathematics or one subject in general studies (humanities and natural sciences).

---

[17] Class teachers are those who teach a class in grades 1–6 in basic education. Subject teachers are those who teach only a discipline or specialized area in grades 7–9 in basic education and at upper secondary school.

Students may include optional tests. The Matriculation Examination may also be taken by students in vocational upper secondary education and training.

- Tertiary education consists of two complementary sectors: Universities and Polytechnics (also called Universities of Applied Sciences, providing both theoretical knowledge and practical skills). Universities are independent corporations under Public Law or Foundations under Private Law. About 64 % of their budgets are directly funded by the Government. Polytechnics are municipal or private institutions, subject to governmental authorization.
- The education system has no dead ends, and adult education is also available at all levels. More than 1.7 million adults participate in different types of adult education each year.

Education is free at all levels, from pre-primary to higher education. This includes, at pre-primary and basic education levels, transportation, textbooks, meals, comprehensive health care, including dental care and psychological support, guidance and counselling, and special education services. At the secondary level and in higher education, the books are not free, but a free meal is provided at the secondary level. Responsibility for educational funding is divided between the State and local authorities.

Only about 1 % of schools providing basic education are private, accounting for around 2 % of all their pupils. Private schools are not allowed to collect student fees (with some exceptions), but publicly supervised private schools generally receive State aid according to the same principles as other schools.

> Today, Finland is a wealthy Nordic welfare state with zero illiteracy, low infant mortality, high productivity and relatively high taxes. A major aspect of societal income distribution is investment in education which is free-of-charge from the pre-school year at age 6 to tertiary education, and accessible to all regardless of language, ethnicity, gender, or social status. Basic education is a combination of centralised and decentralised management and the private sector is very limited due to both historical reasons and a general trust in the high standard of the municipal schools. (Kupiainen et al. 2009, pp. 49, 50)

Finnish public education is inspired and aims at cultivating values that may be synthesized as follows.

• Values and Principles of the Public Education

- *Humanism and universalism*
- *Equity and inclusion*
- *Differentiation and decentralization*
- *Trust and responsibility*

The Basic Education Act 628/1998 (Amendments up to 1136/2010), Section 2 (Objectives of education),[18] provides the statements:

---

[18] www.finlex.fi/en/laki/kaannokset/1998/en19980628.pdf.

1. The purpose of education referred to in this Act is to support pupils' growth into humanity and into ethically responsible membership of society and to provide them with knowledge and skills needed in life. Furthermore, the aim of pre-primary education, as part of early childhood education, is to improve children's capacity for learning.
2. Education shall promote civilisation and equality in society and pupils' prerequisites for participating in education and otherwise developing themselves during their lives.
3. The aim of education shall further be to secure adequate equity in education throughout the country.

According to the National Core Curriculum for Basic Education 2004 (2.1 Underlying values of basic education)[19]: "The underlying values of basic education are human rights, equality, democracy, natural diversity, preservation of environmental viability, and the endorsement of multiculturalism. Basic education promotes responsibility, a sense of community, and respect for the rights and freedoms of the individual". These values "are to be incorporated into the objectives and contents of basic education, and into everyday activity". The Core Curriculum includes seven "Cross-curricular themes" to approach "the educational challenges of the time", which should be "included in the core and optional subjects and in joint events such as assemblies, and are to be manifest in the school's operational culture" (7.1). The first two are "Growth as a person" and "Cultural identity and internationalism". The objectives of the first are the following (7.1.1):

The pupils will

- come to understand their physical, psychological and social growth, and their uniqueness as individuals
- learn to evaluate the ethics of their actions and to recognize right and wrong
- learn to recognize the importance of aesthetic experiences to the quality of life
- learn to recognize their individual learning styles and develop themselves as learners
- learn to function as members of a group and community

The core contents of the second are as follows (7.1.2):

- one's own culture, the culture of one's home region, and the nature of being Finnish, Nordic and European
- mother cultures and multiculturalism
- human rights and prerequisites for trust, mutual respect, and successful cooperation among human groups
- internationalism in different spheres of life, and skills for functioning in international interaction
- the importance of the culture of manners

One of the objectives of the third cross-curricular theme (media skills and communication) reads: "take a critical stance towards contents conveyed by the media, and to ponder the related values of ethics and aesthetics in communication" (7.1.3).

The Core Curriculum also includes Ethics as alternative to Religion, an objective of which is to "gain an introduction to the principles of human rights, tolerance, justice, and sustainable development, and learn to assume responsibility for

---

[19] www.oph.fi/english/curricula_and_qualifications/basic_education.

themselves, other people, the community, and nature" (7.12). It is "a multidisci-plinary whole in terms of its foundation" whose rich contents include "The community and human rights, namely":

- foundations of living together, rules, agreements, promises, trust, honesty and fairness, the Golden Rule
- rights of children, right and obligation, human rights
- equality, peace, democracy, the world of the future
- foundations of ethics, moral justification of action, purpose and consequence of action
- my own life's ethical problems solutions

It further includes "ethics of human rights, environmental ethics", as well as "my future, acting for the future's sake". In this connection, it should be highlighted that, on 26 September 2013, the Ministry commissioned a report to examine how democracy and human rights objectives are implemented and their content is processed in teacher training in universities and polytechnics. The report concluded that, while democracy and human rights are seen in all units as key values in education, much more should be done. It made a number of recommendations on teacher education and teacher training for making democracy and participation more visible and better incorporated into the education of teachers. This requires, in particular, that resources are targeted towards research on democracy and human rights education.[20]

The Ethics assessment criteria mention:

- know the main features of human and civil rights and be capable of explaining the difference between them […]
- be able to explain the mutual dependence between rights and responsibilities […]
- recognize violations of human and civil rights and know how to evaluate the bases of various demands for equality and rights
- know about problems of contemporary society and be able to present both optimistic and pessimistic outlooks on the future

Sahlberg (2011) highlights:

> Equity in education is an important feature in Nordic welfare states. It means more than just opening access to an equal education for all. Equity in education is a principle that aims at guaranteeing high quality education for all in different places and circumstances. In the Finnish context equity is about having a socially fair and inclusive education system that is based on equality of educational opportunities.
> […]
> The Finnish education system follows the principle of inclusiveness regarding the treatment of students with differing characteristics and needs. […]
> The equitable Finnish education system is a result of systematic attention to social justice and early intervention to help those with special needs, and close interplay between education and other sectors – particularly health and social sectors – in Finnish society. (pp. 45, 69)

In his opinion, "if I had to pick up one thing that Finland is doing particularly systematically and well to enhance equity, it's the special education system. It's

---

[20] www.minedu.fi/OPM/Julkaisut/2014/Demokratia_ja_ihmisoikeudet.html?lang=en.

.

very pricey, it's very expensive. But when we do our economics of education, we also calculate that the cost of not doing that would be much higher later on".[21] Special needs should be identified and met as early as possible in order to prevent their worsening and cumulative effects.

Following the Amendments and Additions to the National Core Curriculum for Basic Education (3.4)[22]:

> Differentiation of instruction is a primary means of taking the needs of the teaching groups and the diversity of pupils into account, permeating through all instruction. […] Each pupil is guided to learn in the way that suits him or her best. Pupils' interests are taken into account in instruction by linking the knowledge and skills being learnt to experiences and activities that they find meaningful.

Another feature of the Finnish education system is decentralization. It is largely decentralized and municipalized (there are 446 municipalities). Schools can be municipal, inter-municipal (cooperation between municipalities) or private but subject to governmental approval. Each school is usually managed by a board where teachers, non-teaching staff, students and parents are represented. Comprehensive schools, upper secondary schools and vocational institutions draw their curricula based on the National Core Curriculum issued by the National Board of Education. Teachers and schools are responsible for assessing student performance, there being only one national assessment: the Matriculation Examination, at the end of general upper secondary school that is the only external national test in the Finnish education system.

> Much of what has been previously noted is possible only if parents, students, and authorities trust teachers and school principals. The Finnish education system was highly centralised until the early 1990s. Schools were strictly regulated by the central agencies; a dense network of rules and orders governed the daily work of teachers. The gradual shift towards trusting schools and teachers began in the late 1980s. In the early 1990s, the era of a trust-based school culture formally started in Finland.
> The culture of trust means that education authorities and political leaders believe that teachers, together with principals, parents and their communities, know how to provide the best possible education for their children and youth. Trust can only flourish in an environment that is built upon honesty, confidence, professionalism and good governance. (OECD 2012, p. 100)

Consequently, as an OECD Report (2011b) notes: "As with all education systems that achieve good results, Finland's success is a function of the interaction of several different factors that work together to create a coherent approach that supports consistent system-wide performance" (p. 123). They compose an alchemy whose main ingredients may be summarized as follows.

---

[21] Retrieved June 2014 from https://theconversation.edu.au/finnish-education-guru-pasi-sahlberg-in-conversation-full-transcript-9836.

[22] www.oph.fi/download/132551_amendments_and_additions_to_national_core_curriculum_basic_education.pdf.

• **Explaining the "Finnish Education Miracle"**

- *Education reform: consensus, vision, wholeness, depth*
- *Education quality: reflex and ferment of social quality*
- *Welcoming and well-equipped schools*
- *Less can be better*
- *Teaching profession: at the heart of the education quality*

Following Sahlberg (2011):

> As this book illustrates, there is no single reason why any educational system succeeds or fails. Instead, there is a network of interrelated factors – educational, political and cultural – that function differently in different situations. I would, however, like to cite three important elements of Finnish educational policies since the early 1970s that appear to transcend cultures. The first one is an inspiring vision of what good public education should be. Finland has been particularly committed to building a good publicly financed and locally governed basic school for every child. This common educational goal became so deeply rooted in politics and public services in Finland that it survived opposing political governments and ministries unharmed and intact. […]
> As a consequence, the basic values and the main vision of education as public service have remained unchanged since the 1970s. (pp. 6, 131)

It has been "a longer-term vision", built upon "strategic principles, such as equal opportunity for all and putting learning before teaching. Rather than seeking short-term gains education development has focused on consolidating these basic values in education" (Aho et al. 2006, p. 3). Indeed: "There have been over 20 different ministers of education and government coalitions since the 1970s in Finland, but the main principles of education policy have changed little".[23]

A far-reaching vision implies that extensive education reform does not consist in "doing more of the same", as well as "that educational change should be systematic and coherent, in contrast with the current haphazard intervention efforts of many other countries" (Sahlberg 2011, pp. 62, 132).

The education system being a sub-system of cultural–sociopolitical–economic systems, their interplay generates a circle that may be vicious or virtuous.

> Education policies are necessarily interwined with other social policies, and with the overall political culture of a nation. […]
> Finland has a competitive national economy, low levels of corruption, good quality of life, a strong sustainable-development lifestyle, and gender equality. […]
> [E]ducation system performance has to be seen in the context of other systems in the society, for example, health, environment, rule of law, governance, economy, and technology. It is not only that the education system functions well in Finland, but that it is part of a well-functioning democratic welfare state. Attempts to explain the success of the education system in Finland should be put in the wider context and seen as a part of the overall function of democratic civil society. […] The quality of a nation or its parts is rarely a result of any single factor. The entire society needs to perform harmoniously. (pp. 39, 96, 115)

---

[23] http://pasisahlberg.com/finlands-educational-success-is-no-miracle.

Consequently, the Finnish education system holds the pedigree of the Nordic *Welfare State* and the sociocultural and political *ethos* of Finland as a country that also regularly features in other international rankings: good governance, justice, health, security, freedom, environment, well-being, corruption, etc.

Sahlberg notes that:

> Another overlooked direction of Finnish educational development is reform of school architecture along the guidelines set out by the National Curriculum Framework and its pedagogical and philosophical principles. [...] Physical environment provides an important context for both students and teachers. [...] The school building can create a sense of well-being, respect, and happiness – all hallmarks of Finnish school. (p. 128)

As the Amendments and Additions to the National Core Curriculum for Basic Education[24] reads: "The school community should be safe, friendly and respectful in terms of atmosphere" (2.3), and learning should be meaningful in order to "stimulate a desire to learn" (3.4).

Furthermore, the desire to go and to be in school is not nourished with overloading work and the pressure of standardized tests. According to the Basic Education Act 628/1998 (Amendments up to 1136/2010), Section 24.1 (Pupil's work load)[25]: "The pupil's work load in basic education must be such as to allow him or her enough time for rest, recreation and hobbies over and above the time spent in school, school travel and homework". In this regard, Robert Schwartz said that Finland "is a wonderful case study. Kids start school later; school hours are shorter than most others; they don't assign homework; their teachers are in front of kids less" (as cit. in Pearson 2012, p. 41). The Finnish school proves that *less can be better*.

Last but not least, as Sahlberg (2011) wrote:

> Many factors contributed to Finland's educational system's current fame, such as its 9-year comprehensive school (peruskoulu) for all children, modern learning-focused curricula, systematic care for students with diverse special needs, and local autonomy and shared responsibility. However, research and experience suggest that one factor trumps all others: the daily contributions of excellent teachers. [...] Finnish experience shows that it is more important to ensure that teachers' work in schools is based on professional dignity and social respect so that they can fulfill their intention of selecting teaching as lifetime careers. [...]
>
> Indeed, Finns continue to regard teaching as a noble, prestigious profession – akin to physicians, lawyers, or economists – driven mainly by moral purpose, rather than by material interest, careers, or rewards.
> [...]
> Due to the popularity of teaching and becoming a teacher, only Finland's best and most commited are able to realize those professional dreams. [...] Annually, only about 1 of every 10 applicants will be accepted to prepare to become a teacher in Finnish primary schools. [...]

---

[24] www.oph.fi/download/132551_amendments_and_additions_to_national_core_curriculum_basic_education.pdf.

[25] www.finlex.fi/en/laki/kaannokset/1998/en19980628.pdf.

Thus, I call this phenomenon the 'Finnish advantage', while other nations continue to wonder how to get the 'best and brightest' into teaching.
[…]
A critical condition for attracting the most able young people year after year to teacher education, however, is that a teacher's work should represent an independent and respectful profession rather than merely focus on technical implementation of externally mandated standards, endless tests, and administrative burdens. (pp. 70, 71, 73, 76, 95)

In short: "Teachers in Finland are representatives of a high-quality academic and ethical profession" (Niemi 2012, p. 35). Their quality is constructed and cultivated through a global approach embracing all aspects of the teaching profession: selection, education, independence, work conditions, pay, etc. As a consequence: "Parents trust teachers as professionals who know what is best for their children" (Sahlberg 2011, p. 129).

An OECD publication (2011b) comments:

The fact that there seems to be very little interest in Finland in instituting the assessment and external accountability regimes that have characterised the reform strategies of many OECD countries, most prominently the US and the UK, is perhaps the best evidence of the fundamental trust that seems to exist between the educators and the community. Given the extraordinary performance of the Finnish system over the past decade, this is a lesson others might want to study. (p. 131)

All in all, Finland's education system is an example of a human rights approach to education quality.

• **Right to Education: The Secret**

The secret of the *Finnish Educational Miracle* is the *right to education* as a fundamental right and global public good that is everyone's right to every education he or she is entitled to, while respecting all their human rights.

The Finnish Constitution states: "Everyone has the right to basic education free of charge" (Section 16—Educational rights).[26] The Amendments and Additions to the National Core Curriculum for Basic Education[27] repeat: "Every pupil has a right to high-quality education as well as an opportunity to receive guidance and support for learning and schooling on all school days" (4.1). Earlier, it had been recalled: "Finland has also committed to international agreements, programmes and declarations which require provision of education so as to guarantee learning for children and young people at a common school for all" (2.3). Sahlberg (2011) remarks: "Education in Finland is widely seen as a public good and is therefore protected as a basic human right to all in the Constitution" (p. 10).

As a consequence, if the *habitat* of the *Finnish Educational Miracle* is not exportable, its principles are nevertheless universally realizable. They meet the principles of the Ethics of the Right to Education—embedded in the Ethics of

---

[26] www.finlex.fi/fi/laki/kaannokset/1999/en19990731.pdf.

[27] www.oph.fi/download/132551_amendments_and_additions_to_national_core_curriculum_basic_education.pdf.

Human Rights and drawing on the Ethics of the Rights of the Child—that may be thus stated:

- *Primacy of the best interests of the holder of the right to education*
- *Full development of the human personality*
- *Respect for the dignity and rights of the child*
- *Priority of human rights education as an ethical, civic and international education*

These principles attempt to synthesize the normative content of the right to education that is a complex of rights: those formally recognized as elements of its core content, or implicit in its scope, or concerning the conditions of its implementation.

The Finnish school is a school of the right to education because it is an institution centred on each child or adolescent as a unique human being who has an indefinite potential and a need to learn, to learn to learn, to learn to be—to be human and to live humanely together with other human beings, close or distant. It is a school of liberty, creativity, responsibility and universality. "Purpose of schooling has focused on holistic development of personality that includes knowledge, skills, values, creativity and interpersonal characteristics" (Aho et al. 2006, p. 3).

As we saw, Finnish education politics does not overlook the deep interdependence existing between the right to education and other human rights, both of children and of their parents, including a broad conception of the right to human rights education. The National Core Curriculum for Basic Education includes many references to human rights and the rights of the child.

In sum, education is a real national priority, both as "a moral and economic imperative", as Sahlberg (2011) wrote. "Governments from the political left and right have respected education as the key public service for all citizens and maintained their belief that only a highly and widely educated nation will be successful in world markets" (pp. 1, 130).

Other principles of the *Finnish Educational Miracle* are not new either. The merit of Finnish reformers was rather to want and to know how to apply, with creativity and consistency, principles borrowed from the universal pedagogic heritage, such as the following:

- *Individualization and participation as methodological principles*
- *Autonomy and responsibility as higher values of education*
- *Desire as the drive of learning*

As we know, centring the learning process in the learner and making it active was a common feature of the "new schools" which the New Education Movement gave rise to during the first half of the twentieth century. These principles were closely related to those of autonomy and responsibility promoted through the democratic participation of children and adolescents in school governance. Autonomy may be considered as the highest expression of the free and full development of the human personality. It implies the consciousness of, and capacity for, responsibility as the highest expression of human morality.

Another principle underlying Finnish education politics and pedagogy seems to be one that is the most neglected by education reformers and professionals worldwide. It was highlighted by Jean-Jacques Rousseau (1712–1778) when he said in *Émile* (1762) that the best method is "one which is generally overlooked—it consists in the desire to learn. Arouse this desire in your scholar […] any method will serve" (1993a, Book II, p. 96). Indeed, while the human being has needs, it is essentially a being of desires. The child learns only what he or she desires to know, with whom he or she likes to learn, and where he or she feels well. This is critical for any human future.

• **Conclusion**

Finland is probably the most harmoniously developed country in the world. Education has been the engine of its high global well-being.

> After World War II, the idea was to provide all Finns with an equal opportunity for good public education regardless of their domicile, socioeconomic status, or other life conditions. This became the main principle in building *peruskoulu* in the early 1970s. The first PISA survey in 2000 proved that the Finnish Big Dream was fulfilled. (Sahlberg 2011, pp. 139, 140)

Peruskoulu (common basic school) reaches far beyond the PISA boundaries, as indicated earlier.

> Comprehensive schools that offer all children the same top quality, publicly financed education – not only excellent teaching but counseling, health, nutrition and special-education services as well – seems to play a key role in building a high-performing education system. Good school for all, not for some, is the core value that drives education in Finland. (Aho et al. 2006, p. 2)

The Finnish common basic school is probably the best in the world. It epitomizes the compatibility between equity and quality, inclusiveness and competitiveness, so making more evident, by contrast, how miserable neoliberal education politics is.

However, success may have mollifying effects (as the Nokia case illustrates) or be contaminated by neoliberal pressures (funding for primary schools has been cut, for example). In any case, human education is never a finished endeavour: it is a work in progress because societies transform and change, and new challenges arise.[28]

---

[28] In this connection, a UK Report notices:

> The transition from an industrial society to a knowledge society has brought about an unprecedented level of wealth, meaning that people can move beyond thinking about survival to thinking about their subjective well-being.
>
> Values have shifted from an emphasis on physical and economic well-being to individual freedom and self-expression (amongst others).
>
> This new focus on subjective well-being is combined with unparalleled availability of information due to the exponential growth of technology in the past quarter of a century. (Spada 2009, p. 6).

Therefore, the Finnish Government has launched in February 2014 a national report entitled "The Future School of Finland: A New Beginning".[29]

To resist the neoliberal winds blowing over the world (which are more gelid than the Nordic winter) and not breaking but rather deepening the virtuous circle of the right to education school that has it been so wise to create—here is Finland's historic responsibility towards its children and future, and, in addition, as an example, towards all children of the world and the future of Humankind.[30]

References

Aho, E., Pitkänen, K., & Sahlberg, P. (2006). *Policy development and reform principles of basic and secondary education in Finland since 1968.* Washington: The World Bank, Education Working Paper Series, No 2. http://siteresources.worldbank.org/EDUCATION/Resources/278200-1099079877269/547664-1099079967208/Education_in_Finland_May06.pdf

Anderson, L. (2004). *Increasing teacher effectiveness.* Paris: UNESCO, International Institute for Educational Planning. http://unesdoc.unesco.org/images/0013/001376/137629e.pdf

Asia Society. (2011). *The international summit on the teaching profession—Improving teacher quality around the world.* http://asiasociety.org/files/lwtw-teachersummitreport0611.pdf

Asia Society. (2012). *The 2012 international summit on the teaching profession—Teaching and leadership for the twenty-first century.* http://asiasociety.org/files/2012teachingsummit.pdf

Asia Society. (2014). *The 2013 international summit on the teaching profession—Excellence, equity, and inclusiveness—High quality teaching for all.* http://asiasociety.org/files/2014teachingsummit.pdf

Barber, M., Donnelly, K., & Rizvi, S. (2012). *Oceans of innovation—The Atlantic, the Pacific, global leadership and the future of education.* London: Institute of Public Policy Research. (www.ippr.org/images/media/files/publication/2012/09/oceans-of-innovation_Aug2012_9543.pdf)

Barber, M., & Mourshed, M. (2007). *How the world's best-performing school systems come out on top.* McKinsey and Company. www.mckinsey.com/locations/UK_Ireland/~/media/Reports/UKI/Education_report.ashx

Bourdoncle, R. (1993). La professionnalisation des enseignants: les limites d'un mythe. *Revue Française de Pédagogie, 105,* 83–119.

---

[29] The process is steered by a broad-based group chaired by the Minister of Education and Science that includes representatives from eight political parties; delegates from the Ministry of Education and Culture and the Finnish National Board of Education; four to five representatives from research fields, who are also members in the theme area working groups; delegates from the Trade Union of Education in Finland, the Association of Finnish Principals, the Association of Finnish Independent Education Employers, the Trade Union for the Public and Welfare Sectors, the Association of Finnish; involvement of Local and Regional Authorities, the Finnish Parents' League and secondary school student organizations.

The steering group coordinates two working groups focusing on the following themes: 1) the significance of competence and learning in terms of societal development, and 2) motivation for learning, school satisfaction and teaching arrangements and methods. (See: www.minedu.fi/OPM/Tiedotteet/2014/02/perusopetus.html?lang=en).

[30] *The Future is Finnish*—such was the title of a text published on the *Newsweek* website on May 23, 1999... (www.newsweek.com/future-finnish-166786).

Darling-Hammond, L., & Rothman, R. (2011). Lessons learned from Finland, Ontario, and Singapore. In L. Darling-Hammond, & R. Rothman (Ed.), *Teacher and leader effectiveness in high-performing education systems* (pp. 1–11). Washington, DC: Alliance for Excellent Education and Stanford Center for Opportunity Policy in Education. www.all4ed.org/files/TeacherLeaderEffectivenessReport.pdf

European Commission. (2012). *Supporting the teaching professions for better learning outcomes.* Commission Staff Working Document—Accompanying the Document: Communication from the Commission—Rethinking Education: Investing in skills for better socio-economic outcomes (SWD (2012) 374 final). Retrieved July 2014 from http://eur-lex.europa.eu/LexUriServ/LexUriServ.do?uri=SWD:2012:0374:FIN:EN:PDF

Ginsburg, M., & Megahed, N. (2009). Comparative perspectives on teachers, teaching and professionalism. In L. Saha, & A. Dworkin (Ed.), *International handbook of research on teachers and teaching* (pp. 539–556). Berlin: Springer.

Kant, I. (1803). *On education* ('Über Pädagogik', Translated by Annette Churton, with an Introduction by C. A. Foley Rhys Davids, M.A.). Boston: D. C. Heath and Co., Publishers, 1906. http://archive.org/details/kantoneducationu00kantuoft

Kupiainen, S., Hautamäki, J., & Karjalainen, T. (2009). *The Finnish education system and PISA.* Helsinki: Ministry of Education. www.minedu.fi/export/sites/default/OPM/Julkaisut/2009/liitteet/opm46.pdf?lang=en

LeCompte, M. (2009). Trends in research on teaching: An historical and critical overview. In L. Saha, & A. Dworkin (Ed.), *International handbook of research on teachers and teaching* (pp. 25–60). Berlin: Springer.

Leslie, Ch. (Ed.). (2013). *Towards a royal college of teaching—Raising the status of the profession.* London: The Royal College of Surgeons of England. Retrieved July 2014 from http://filestore.aqa.org.uk/news/pdf/AQA-NEWS-TOWARDS-A-ROYAL-COLLEGE.PDF

MacBeath, J. (2012). *Future of teaching profession.* Education International Research Institute, University of Cambridge—Faculty of Education, Leadership for Learning—The Cambridge Network. http://download.ei-ie.org/Docs/WebDepot/EI%20Study%20on%20the%20Future%20of%20Teaching%20Profession.pdf

National Center on Education and the Economy. (2007). *Tough choices or tough times—The Report of the New Commission on the Skills of the American Workforce—Executive Summary,* Washington. www.skillscommission.org/wp-content/uploads/2010/05/ToughChoices_EXECSUM.pdf

Niemi, H. (2012). The societal factors contributing to education and schooling in Finland. In N. Niemi, & A. Toom, & A. Kallioniemi (Ed.), *Miracle of education—The principles and practices of teaching and learning in finnish schools* (pp. ix–xi, 19–38). Rotterdam: Sense Publishers.

OECD. (1990). *L'enseignant aujourd'hui —Fonctions, Statut, Politiques.* OECD Publishing.

OECD. (2005). *Teachers matte—Attracting, developing and retaining effective teachers.* OECD Publishing.

OECD. (2011a). *Building a high-quality teaching profession—Lessons from around the world—Background Report for the International Summit on the Teaching Profession.* OECD Publishing. Retrieved January 2013 from www2.ed.gov/about/inits/ed/internationaled/background.pdf

OECD. (2011b). *Strong performers and successful reformers in education—Lessons from PISA for the United States.* OECD Publishing. Retrieved June 2014 from www.oecd.org/pisa/46623978.pdf

OECD. (2012). *Strong performers and successful reformers in education—Lessons from PISA for Japan.* OECD Publishing. Retrieved June 2014 from www.oecd.org/edu/school/programmeforinternationalstudentassessmentpisa/49802616.pdf

OECD. (2014). *Equity, excellence and inclusiveness in education—Policy lessons from around the world.* OECD Publishing, by Andreas Schleicher. Retrieved June 2014 from http://teachfirstnz.org/images/uploads/Documents/OECD.pdf

Parliament of the Commonwealth of Australia. (1998). *A class act—Inquiry into the status of the teaching profession*. Canberra: Senate Employment, Education and Training Reference Committee. www.aph.gov.au/ ~ /media/wopapub/senate/committee/eet_ctte/completed_inquiries/1996_99/teachers/report/report_pdf.ashx

Pearson. (2012). *Lessons in country performance in education—2012 Report*. London: The Learning Curve, Economist Intelligence Unit. http://thelearningcurve.pearson.com/the-report

Pochard, M. (2008). *Livre Vert sur l'évolution du métier d'enseignant—Rapport au ministre de l'Éducation nationale*. Paris: La documentation Française. Retrieved January 2013 from http://lesrapports.ladocumentationfrancaise.fr/BRP/084000061/0000.pdf

Rousseau, J.-J. (1993a). *Émile* (Translated by Barbara Foxley, Introduction by P. D. Jimack). Vermont: Everyman (2004).

Saha, J., & Dworkin, A. (Ed.). (2009). *International handbook of research on teachers and teaching*. Berlin: Springer.

Sahlberg, P. (2011). *Finnish lessons: What can the world learn from educational change in Finland*. New York: Teachers College Press.

Spada. (2009). *British professions today: The state of the sector.* www.ukipg.org.uk/executive_group_resources/spada-british-professions-today.pdf

Part II
Professionality of Teachers

Chapter 4
Sociology of the Professions

Abstract The Sociology of the Professions is a domain within the Sociology of Work whose object is the study of professions as a special category of occupations. The distinction between "profession" and "occupation"—its Anglo-Saxon starting point—is thus understood: while the term "occupation" means every activity, work, function or job that is the main source of someone's livelihood, the term "profession" distinguishes a more or less specialized, well-paid and prestigious occupation. The main approaches and theories in the field of the Sociology of the Professions are the following: functionalist ("trait approach"), interactionist ("process approach") and conflict ("power approach"). I submit that every lawful occupation, by means of which individuals earn their principal regular income, is their profession, with its corresponding utility and dignity, whatever its reality. Nevertheless, while a case may be made for considering the distinction between profession and occupation as a socially elitist construct, there are objective differences and social differentiation among occupations/professions. Occupations distinguish themselves by their level of professionality (or professionhood). Professionalism is a more frequently used word, but their distinction and definitions are not well-established in the sociological literature. As understood here, professionality means the global profile of a profession, that is, everything distinguishing it from other occupational groups; professionalism means the practice of a profession according to its identity content, as described in Professional Standards. Ultimately, professionalism amounts to the unity of science, conscience and excellence. Professional Standards are principally standards for professional fitness, competence, education, practice and conduct. They should form the normative framework essential for accreditation of initial and continuing education, for registration and certification, for any possible disciplinary sanction, as well as for the periodic evaluation of performance. Another relevant sociological concept is that of professional self-regulation. It will be the focus of the third part of this study.

Keywords Sociology of the Professions · Profession · Professionality · Professionalism · Professional Standards

© The Author(s) 2015   47
A. Reis Monteiro, *The Teaching Profession*, SpringerBriefs in Education,
DOI 10.1007/978-3-319-12130-7_4

Alexander M. Carr-Saunders and Paul A. Wilson, in their classic study on *The Professions* (1933), added to the *big three* professions (*Divinity*, *Law*, *Medicine*, mentioned by Joseph Addison in an essay written in 1711) the military and education. Nevertheless, they concluded that teaching was not a true profession because teachers were mainly public servants entirely controlled by the State. For Amitai Etzioni, it is a "semi-profession", but in Talcott Parsons' opinion, teachers are professionals.

"There have been debates over the years and throughout nations as to whether teachers are professionals as opposed to mere 'workers', and whether teaching is a profession and not just an 'occupation' (Hoyle 1995)" (Villegas-Reimers 2003, p. 33). Teachers' professional identity remains controversial, "even when most of the literature nowadays is focusing on the perception of teachers as professionals" (p. 36). That is why, as Mark Ginsburg and Nagwa Megahed (2009) note, "historically and today 'profession', 'professionalization', and 'professionalism' have punctuated the discourses about reforming teaching, teachers, and teacher education around the world (Barton et al. 1994; Furlong 1992; Ginsburg 1987b; Gottlieb and Cornbleth 1989; Herbst 1989; Yeom 2005)" (p. 548).

> Although answers to this question have varied somewhat, studies of the occupation of teaching in *Africa* (Bagunywa, 1975; Nagwu, 1977), *Asia* (Kale, 1970; Koo, 2002; Levine, 1969; White, 1981), *Europe* (Hargreaves, 1980; Helsby, 1995; Hoyle, 1974; Legatt, 1970; Pritchard, 1983), *Latin America* (Alba, 1969; Imaz Gispert and Salinas Alvarez, 1984), *the Middle East* (Mazawi, 1994; Reid, 1974), and *North America* (Darling-Hammond, 1990; Dreeben, 1970; Howsam, 1980; Lieberman, 1956; Lortie, 1975) have generally concluded that teaching cannot be considered as a fully developed profession, but rather as semi-profession or aspiring profession. (p. 540)[1]

In this regard, Richard M. Ingersoll and David Perda (2008) wrote too: "Clearly, teaching continues to be treated as, at best, a 'semi-profession' (Lortie 1969, 1975)" (p. 116). Reagan (2010) remarks: "The problem, from a philosophical and conceptual perspective, is that we lack clarity about what it means to be a 'professional'", as well as "the lack of a clear and coherent definition of what we really mean by 'professionalism'".

Before approaching the main aspects concerning teaching as a profession, a short outlook of the landscape of the Sociology of the Professions may be useful, as well as clarifying some concepts.

4.1 Origins and Main Theories

As Robert Dingwall (2008) observes, technological progress may render ancient occupations obsolete (for instance, as a result of the invention of new building materials), and new ones come on stage (the electrician, for instance, in the nineteenth century). In addition, "as societies develop, work becomes more complex

---

[1] For example: "The evidence gathered during the Review is unequivocal: while teachers are most often described as professional people, teaching is not a profession" (Ramsey 2000, p. 94).

and the division of labor more specialized through the dissection of occupations" (p. 46). The advent of the nation states, the development of the capitalist economy, the scientific technological progress and the emergence of the modern professions are linked events. The major professions, such as Medicine and Law, achieved their privileged status in the second half of the nineteenth century. Most contemporary professions are a twentieth-century phenomenon, with the increasing specialization of knowledge and expansion of technology.

Following Dingwall, social scientists "have been fascinated by the professions" as a category of occupations, and their analyses "were broadly appreciative and sympathetic" (p. 77), because of the particular value of their services. So did, for example, Adam Smith (1723–1790), Herbert Spencer (1820–1903) and Thomas H. Marshall (1893–1981), in UK; the Harvard Sociology inspired by Talcott E. F. Parsons (1902–1979) and the Chicago Sociology of Everett Ch. Hughes (1897–1983), in the USA; Émile Durkheim (1858–1917) in France; and Max Weber (1864–1920) in Germany.

The distinction between *profession* and *occupation* is the starting point of the Anglo-Saxon Sociology of the Professions that Andrew Abbot defined as a domain within the Sociology of Work whose object is the study of professions. The distinction is so understood: the term "occupation" means every activity, work, function or job that is the main source of someone's livelihood; the term "profession" distinguishes a more or less specialized, well-paid and prestigious occupation, whose models are Medicine and Law as *learned professions*—a term whose meaning goes back to the Middle Ages, when it was connoted with Divinity, Law and Medicine. The intermediate occupations—more than mere occupations, but not possessing all traits of professions—were called "semi-professions", "quasi-professions", "sub-professions", or "pseudo-professions".

In Dingwall's opinion, the founders of the Sociology of the Professions were Parsons (with his critique of utilitarian Economics in *The Structure of Social Action*, 1937) and Hughes (whose teaching was collected in *The Sociological Eye*, 1971). Parsons focused less on the professions in his later writings, but they remained central in Hughes' work. After World War I, but principally in the second half of the twentieth century, the demand for professional status grew more and more, and the professions became the subject of varied research.

The concept of a profession raises three main questions: What really distinguishes professions from other occupations? Why and how only some occupations succeed in gaining professional statute, particularly outside of the Anglo-Saxon world? In the times of neoliberalism and globalization, what future may professions have, as we know them?

The main approaches/theories in the field of the Sociology of the Professions are the functionalist, the interactionist and the conflict ones.

The functionalist approach—the *standard model*—is also known as the attributes or taxonomic approach. It is a functionalist approach because it stems from sociological functionalism (the theory that analyses social facts in the light of their function in terms of the conservation of society as a whole); it is an attributes approach because it tries to identify the attributes or traits that distinguish professions from other occupations; it is a taxonomic approach because it classifies occupations according to the attributes characterizing them.

The origin of the functionalist/attributes/taxonomic approach is associated with A. Flexner's ground-breaking paper "Is social work a profession?", published in the USA in 1915 (*Proceedings of the National Conference of Charities and Correction*). He proposed a definition that became canonical, following which a profession distinguishes itself by six attributes: it performs a duty of great responsibility, has a theoretical knowledge base, aims at solving practical problems, its knowledge base is transmissible by means of systematic teaching, tends to self-organize in associations, and has a service ideal. In his opinion, an occupation that does not meet all such attributes is a "semi-profession" or "an occupation on the way to professionalization" (as cit. in Dubar and Tripier 2009, p. 3). In the wake of Flexner, attempts were made to develop his professional blueprint. More than twenty attributes were proposed, but without reaching any broad consensus.

This so-called *professional model* prevailed until the 1960s. It is criticized for being an *ideology of professionalism* in line with what George Bernard Shaw (1856–1950) famously wrote in *The Doctor's Dilemma* (1906)[2]: "All professions are conspiracies against the laity" (Sir Patrick, Act I), referring to their methods to acquire wealth, power and prestige.

In the beginning of the 1970s, a movement of new approaches/theories to the professional phenomenon emerged, qualified as interactionist. They withdrew from the distinction between profession and occupation, deeming it to be futile and useless, and took as a principle that a profession is any occupation recognized as such. Their main concept is not that of professional attributes but that of professionalization understood as the dynamic process through which a profession is constructed by those practising it, both collectively and as a way of self-fulfilment. The professionalization process includes successive steps ("escalator model"): the occupation becomes full-time, its knowledge and skills are acquired in proper institutions, associations are created, standards are adopted, and power to licence won. The Sociology of the Professions evolved thus to a Sociology of Professionalization.

Meanwhile, even more diversified approaches/theories were flourishing. They are often denominated conflict approaches/theories. Professions are now seen mainly as actors of the economic field that win the exclusivity of practicing an activity and jurisdiction over its segment of the market of services, monopolizing and closing it. Professional power is examined from neo-Marxist and neo-Weberian points of view.

The three approaches may be, therefore, also identified as "trait approach", "process approach" and "power approach". As the professional phenomenon is undergoing increasing transformation, the discussion is sometimes about *new professionalism, post-professionalism, post-modern professionalism*, etc. In effect, the professional landscape is rapidly changing and the professions have come under

---

[2] www.gutenberg.org/files/5070/5070-h/5070-h.htm.

attack from Governments and the general public. In this connection, a Spada Report (2009) comments:

> Part of the decay in public perceptions of the professions may have been inevitable. Post-industrial values are characterized by declining deference to authority, and political and religious institutions have also suffered in this respect (Inglehart and Baker 2000). The transition from an industrial society to a knowledge society has brought about an unprecedented level of wealth, meaning that people can move beyond thinking about survival to thinking about their subjective well-being. Values have shifted from an emphasis on physical and economic well-being to individual freedom and self-expression (amongst others).
> This new focus on subjective well-being is combined with unparalleled availability of information due to the exponential growth of technology in the past quarter of a century. [...]
> Opinion poll data confirm the professions' gradual erosion in the public opinion. (p. 6)

Indeed, the Internet brought the potential to fill much of the traditional knowledge gap existing between professionals and clients. In addition, older independent professionals, such as doctors and lawyers, now work in employing public, private or professional bureaucratic organizations. Professional services become increasingly commodified, i.e. predominantly treated as products exclusively assessed on the basis of economic criteria. New professions come on stage. Let us borrow from Elizabeth H. Gorman and Rebecca L. Sandefur (2011), at some length, the following synopsis:

> The traditional professions – occupations such as medicine, law, accounting, architecture, the clergy, science and academics, engineering, and a handful of others – enjoyed what was widely recognized as a "golden age" in the middle of the 20th century. (Freidson 2001, p. 182; Galanter and Palay 1991, pp. 20-36) [...]
> The functionalist theoretical orientation that prevailed at the time gave a prominent place to professions as one of the institutions that sustain social order. [...] Scholars devoted a great deal of effort to defining the concepts of *profession* and *professionalism* – and assessing whether or not specific occupations met their definitions – without achieving a clear consensus (Carr-Saunders and Wilson, 1933; Cogan, 1953; Flexner, 1915; Goode, 1969). In the 1960s, scholars began to see all occupations as moving along a continuum of *professionalization* with varying degrees of success (Denzin and Mettlin, 1968; Goode, 1961, 1969; Wilensky, 1964), but the difficulty of defining the ideal type of successful professionalization remained (Becker, 1962).
> Four central attributes of professionalism emerge from this body of scholarship: (a) expert knowledge, (b) technical autonomy, (c) a normative orientation toward the service of others, and (d) high status, income, and other rewards. *Expert knowledge* is the "sine qua non" of professional work. [...]
> In the 1970s, conflict-theory perspectives began to contend that professions achieved status and dominance through their own efforts (Freidson, 1970, 1984) and deliberately sought wealth and power at the expense of other groups (Berlant, 1975). [...]
> Interest in the changing characteristics of professions, especially medicine, grew during the 1970s and 1980s, but many scholars found it difficult to move beyond the intellectual frameworks of the "golden age". [...]
> By the 1990s, many sociologists concluded that existing theoretical frameworks had become implausible and no longer generated interesting questions. Although a trickle of work continued, scholarship with an explicit focus on the professions fell out of fashion and the research area became inactive. [...]

Research on professional and expert work has not vanished. Although the classical sociology of the professions came to an intellectual standstill, the growing importance of professional and knowledge-based work in today's economy made it inevitable that scholars would turn their attention to it once again. They have indeed done so, but the resulting body of work is fragmented across several sociological and interdisciplinary fields. [...]

Four central themes – expert knowledge, autonomy, a normative service orientation supported by community, and high status, income and rewards – provide a strong element of continuity between the classical sociology of the professions and contemporary research. However, these themes reappear today in new forms. [...]

The world of work is increasingly divided into two hemispheres: one which requires expert knowledge accessible only through higher education, and one which does not. Within the knowledge-based hemisphere of work, many of the same questions apply to both traditional professions and occupations of questionable "professional" status. Rather than excluding the latter group of occupations from consideration, current research expands its focus to include them. To the extent that differences remain between traditional professions and other forms of knowledge-based work, this new perspective permits them to be treated as variables in need of explanation – thereby opening the door to many intriguing questions that were previously ruled out of bounds. (pp. 277...281, 284, 290, 291)

The fact remains that:

Professions are involved in every aspect of human life: birth, survival, physical and emotional health, dispute resolution and law-based social order, finance and credit information, educational attainment and socialisation, physical constructs and the built environment, military engagement, peace-keeping and security, entertainment and leisure, religion and our negotiations with the next world. (Olgiati et al. 1998) (Spada 2009, p. 2)

Therefore, according to Dingwall (2008):

- "These do not seem be propitious times for professions", but "obituaries for the professions seem distinctly premature" (pp. 99, 110).
- "There is an unresolved problem at the heart of both the economic and the sociological study of the professions. Are these occupations simple monopolies whose anticompetitive effects distort the social and economic organization of a society or are they institutions which have developed for public interest reasons and should be preserved?" (p. 61).
- "The deregulation of labor markets is said to be a crucial condition for success in the global marketplace and national professions are widely viewed as obstacles to free trade in services" (p. 99). However: "The global order may find that it needs trust-promoting groups much as nation-states did", that is, "global professions" for a globalized word (p. 110).
- Indeed, on the one hand: "The larger in scale and the more complex societies become, the more difficult is to check that the other does indeed have the skills that they claim" (p. 105). On the other hand: "The expansion of information does not make us any more skilled at evaluating it. As we all recognize, the difficult thing is not collecting data but knowing what they mean". As a consequence: "It will be very hard to eliminate intermediaries, whose ability to interpret information and apply it to our case will rest on familiar legitimations.

The professional is our means of reducing uncertainty about important things that we cannot easily or economically verify for ourselves" (p. 108).

- If Eliot Freidson "concluded *Profession of Medicine* [1970] with concerns about a new tyranny of professionalism, *Third Logic* [2001] concludes with a call to sustain the independence of professions as a source of resistance to the greater tyrannies of markets and capital" (p. 139).

4.2 Some Conceptual Options

Profession means, etymologically, a declaration of beliefs or convictions.

Sociologically, while there is a distinction between occupation and profession, so that every profession is an occupation but not every occupation is a profession, there is no single agreed definition of profession as a concept distinct from occupation.

Hughes (1958) wrote: "A profession is an occupation which has attained a special standing among occupations" (p. 157). What are the features or the set of features of such a special standing? This remains a debated issue. All attempts to draw a clear distinction between profession and occupation have been unsuccessful.

The *Guideline for Ethical Practice* (v2.2) of the Association of Professional Engineers and Geologists of Alberta (APEGA 2013) states: "In the generic sense, a profession is a learned calling with specialized knowledge" (p. 2).[3] The Canadian McRuer Report (1968–1971) makes a similar distinction: while professions require "many years of education and training before one is qualified to practice", the educational standards of occupations "are not high, but the emphasis is on technical skill" (p. 1160). However: "Those callings which are customarily thought of as professions cannot be precisely defined" (p. 1161). In Michael Trebilcock's opinion: "An obvious, politically-based definition, albeit of little normative value, would be to accept as professions whatever occupations have been successful in achieving self-regulating status" (as cit. in Spada 2009, p. 9).

In the *Oxford English Dictionary*,[4] the entry "profession" registers "Senses relating to the declaration of faith, principles, etc."; "Senses relating to professional occupation"; and "Senses relating to the office of professor". The latter include the following:

  a. An occupation in which a professed knowledge of some subject, field, or science is applied; a vocation or career, especially one that involves prolonged training and a formal qualification. Also occas. as mass noun: occupations of this kind. In early use applied spec. to the professions of law, the Church, and medicine, and sometimes extended also to the military profession.

---

[3]   www.apega.ca/pdf/Guidelines/GuidelineEthical.pdf.

[4]   www.oed.com/viewdictionaryentry/Entry/152052.

b. More widely: any occupation by which a person regularly earns a living.
c. By profession: by way of an occupation; professionally.
d. The body of people engaged in a particular occupation or calling; sometimes with defining word, as legal, medical, etc.

Consequently, no single feature is sufficiently distinctive of a profession, and the sets of features of professional distinctiveness are varied: specialized knowledge, higher education, extensive training, commitment to service, professional standards, autonomy (not supervised work), self-regulation, strong shared identity, higher social status, etc.

The Resolution Concerning Updating the International Standard Classification of Occupations (ISCO-08),[5] adopted by ILO in 2007, distinguishes between "job" and "occupation". Job is defined "as *a set of tasks and duties performed, or meant to be performed, by one person, including for an employer or in self-employment*"; occupation is defined "as a *set of jobs whose main tasks and duties are characterized by a high degree of similarity*". ISCO-08 develops a system of "major groups", "sub-major groups", "minor groups" and "unit groups". "The basic criteria used to define the system of major, sub-major, minor and unit groups are the 'skill level' and 'skill specialization' required to competently perform the tasks and duties of the occupations". Major groups are ten, one of which is called "Professionals". The Professionals are science and engineering professionals; health professionals; teaching professionals; business and administration professionals; information and communications technology professionals; legal, social and cultural professionals.

Summing up, in most countries, there is no term sociologically equivalent to the English "profession", nor even "liberal profession" that applies to fewer occupations, in particular Medicine, generally considered as the paradigm of professions, and Law.[6] This is one reason why the interest in the Sociology of the Professions in Europe arose only in the late 1990s. In France, for instance, the first publication on *Sociologie des Professions* dates from 1998. The meanings of profession "range

---

[5] www.ilo.org/public/english/bureau/stat/isco/docs/resol08.pdf.

[6] Their characteristics are highlighted in the following definition used by the Netherlands' Council for the Liberal Professions, on its web page:

The liberal profession is conducted on an *individual and (economically) independent* base, on which the individual professionals render *intellectual services* for which they are *responsible (professional autonomy)*. The services are rendered in accordance with the profession's *particular authorities*, the *interests of the clients* involved and the *public interest* (e.g. national health, legal aid). The professional conduct is subjected to national *legislation* or *self-regulatory rules* drafted by the professions' associations that guarantee the *quality, professionalism* and the *fiduciary relationship* between the professional and its clients. The professionals are *monitored* by disciplinary proceedings and are sometimes subjected to governmental supervision. Professionals have completed an *academic education* (and in some cases an additional professional education) and are subject to *permanent education* programs.

Translated in www.eu-newgov.org/database/DELIV/DLTFIbD09d_Final_Chapters_on_self-regulation_The_Netherlands.pdf (p. 46).

from the narrowly defined traditional professions of doctor, lawyer, and accountant to the broadly defined usage as any occupation by which someone earns a living" (Spada 2009, p. 3). The terms profession and occupation are largely used interchangeably.

Dingwall (2008), after noting that profession is a term without a fixed definition, remarks that, although the approach attributes are still dominant, it reached its limits. The emergence of modern professions is "a more complex story". Furthermore, the "liberal professions" are undergoing changes in their classical attributes and their traditional profile is fading. Consequently: "Rather than presupposing the sociological significance of professions as a category, we should be asking what kinds of occupations they are" (pp. 10, 101). Freidson also deems that sociologists should not decree what a profession is, but rather search to examine how the members of a profession "build professionality" (as cit. in Dubar and Tripier 2009, p. 130).

I submit the following views:

- Every lawful occupation, by means of which individuals earn their principal regular income, is their profession, with its corresponding utility and dignity, whatever its reality. Nevertheless, while a case may be made for considering the distinction between profession and occupation as a socially elitist construct, there are objective differences and social differentiation among occupations/ professions.
- We may distinguish three main uses and meanings of the term "profession": a large, an intermediate and a restricted one.

  - In the large sense, profession has a mere economic meaning, designating every occupation aiming to earn one's livelihood.
  - In the intermediate sense, a profession is an occupation consisting in a specific know-how, that is, a functional competence learned empirically or formally (but by short training), exercised in an independent or dependent way. It encompasses the most professional occupations.
  - In the restricted sense, a profession is a highly specialized, well-paid and prestigious occupation.

In other words, the professions distinguish themselves by their level of professionality (or professionhood). Professionality and professionalism are terms whose definitions are not well-established in the sociological literature, being sometimes confused. The following distinction is proposed.

Profissionality is a term of Italian origin (*professionalità*) adopted by other languages: French (*professionnalité*), German (*Professionalität*), Spanish (*profesionalidad*), Portuguese (*profissionalidade*), etc. It may be used to mean the global profile of a profession, that is, everything distinguishing it from other occupational groups. The main factors of the level of professionality are the following:

- *Value of service*, that is, the importance for the individuals and society of the scope of the professional expertise.

- *Identity content*, formed by the knowledge, values and qualities that distinguish a profession and should distinguish its professionals.
- *Professional autonomy*, that is, the independence and responsibility with which the profession may be individually practised and collectively governed.
- *Professional and social status*, which result from the previous factors and are reflected in the income, influence and prestige of the profession.

Professional status and social status are two faces of the same coin: the former consists in the identity content and the autonomy of a profession; the latter means a profession's position within a hierarchy of occupational prestige in a society, resulting both from the value of the service provided and from its professional status.

The level of professionality is, therefore, a *continuum* whose coordinates are the value of the service and the occupation's status. Four levels of professionality may be distinguished:

- *Zero professionality*
  Applies to the lack of professionality of ways of earn a living such as begging or even stealing.
- *Minimum professionality*
  Applies to humble regular occupations deserving some social recognition, such as road sweeper or newspaper seller.
- *Medium professionality*
  Applies to the most common occupations in their functional diversity and social utility.
- *Higher professionality*
  Applies to professions holding the greatest social relevance, responsibility and recognition.

The professions at the highest level of professionality are those which correspond to the ideal type of the professional model. They hold, cumulatively, the following characteristics:

- They provide services that are fundamental for the life, security and general well-being of individuals and society, requiring from their professionals a sense of service that puts the interests of those they serve and the public interest in general over their (legitimate) interests.
- They consist in a particular know-how, with a very specialized and systematized knowledge base, learned through a more or less lengthy theoretical and practical higher education, whose application demands great independence of judgment and decision.
- The power with which their professionals are endowed, resulting from their expertise and independence, with the corresponding responsibility, implies compliance with high Professional Standards of competence, practice and conduct in every professional circumstance.

- They are professions that justify and should deserve the privilege of being self-regulating, that is, to be entrusted with delegated public powers to govern their affairs concerning, in particular, the registration, licensing/certification and professionalism of their members.
- As a consequence of their unique combination of commitment to individual and public service, high expertise, independence, power and responsibility, being generally self-governing, they possess a professional and social status making them more rewarding, attractive and selective.

Such occupations are professions in the densest sociological meaning—*full and true professions*—because each is an "occupational community of shared values as much as of shared expertise" (Dingwall 2008, p. 131), applied at the service of fundamental human rights and needs or providing other services critical for the Common Good. As a consequence, they are professions that we need to trust more than any other, to trust that their power and autonomy are exercised at a high level of intellectual and moral responsibility, i.e. in accordance with demanding Professional Standards of competence, practice and conduct. Because of their social relevance, responsibility and recognition, they carry an inherent ethical, cultural and social dimension indissoluble in the logic of the market of services.

Professionalism is a term with an appeal, not only for practitioners, but also for employers. It entered the managerial literature as a discourse of bureaucratic and hierarchical control of work. Two main uses and meanings of the term may be distinguished:

- It consists in doing well what one does (whatever it may be).
- It consists in doing well something lawful one is supposed to know how to do.

By definition, a profession consists above all in applying specialized knowledge for the resolution/satisfaction of individual and/or collective problems/needs. Professional Standards often include a reference to "good moral character". While it is difficult or impossible to anticipate moral risks, the relevance of a clause pointing to the professionals' moral character is undoubted. According to the McRuer Report (1968–1971): "The requirement of good moral character is to the ethical aspect of a profession what the educational standards are to competence" (p. 1175). Nevertheless, the criterion of who needs and may choose a professional is mainly his or her scientific technical competence, and not so much the (good) person he or she may be. Although one hopes that a good professional be a "good person", a competent professional may not be commendable as person, and a "good person" may not be a competent professional. What is primarily at stake in the practice of a profession is, therefore, the power of its knowledge. As Carr-Saunders and Wilson wrote: "A professional brings asymmetrical knowledge to the service of his client, and thereby exercises power over his client. Therein lie the duties and obligations of a professional to his client" (as cit. in Beaton 2010, p. 9). Professional knowledge endows one with as much power as much it is specialized and the more dangerous the possible consequences of its bad use may be. George Beaton comments:

> Knowledge, as everyone knows, is power. Asymmetrical knowledge between the professional and the client is what gives the professional his or her power over the client – and hence his or her ethical responsibility. [...]
>
> That is why trust is the essence of professionalism and its most necessary component – that around which all the other hallmarks of professionalism revolve. The power that asymmetric knowledge gives one person over another must oblige the practitioner to act in the client's best interests. (pp. 6, 9)

Beaton quotes Freidson who "goes on to say that ethics is the very soul of professionalism" (p. 5). Highlighting the paramountcy of professional independence, Freidson wrote:

> Members of the profession claim the right to judge the demands of employers or patrons and the laws of the state, and to criticize or refuse to obey them. That refusal is based not on personal grounds of individual conscience or desire but on the professional grounds that the basic value or purpose of a discipline is being perverted. [...] Transcendent values add moral substance to the technical content of disciplines. Professionals claim the moral as well as the technical right to control the uses of their discipline (Freidson 2001, pp. 221-222). (p. 19)

For Neil Hamilton (2008) too, professionalism describes "the important elements of an ethical professional identity" (p. 103). But there is still *something else* in professionalism that comes to light from a professional way of being, of standing, of talking, of dressing, etc. In that sense, one could say about professionalism what a Justice of the USA Supreme Court famously said referring to pornography: *I know it when I see it...*[7]

Consequently, professionalism should mean not only to do well what one does, which is a merely instrumental meaning, whose criterion is efficiency, but rather to do well what one can and is expected to do, which is a meaning that adds a normative dimension concerning lawfulness and morality. Its coordinates are then professional expertise and the ethical demand, having as bisector the qualities of professionals. It means, therefore, the practice of a profession according to its identity content as prescribed by the Professional Standards. In sum, ultimately, professionalism amounts to the unity of science, conscience and excellence.

Professional is a term with three principal uses and meanings:

- Whatever job well done is said to be professional, regardless of its lawfulness and value.
- He or she who has a socially recognized occupation that is the regular main source of his or her income is said to be a professional.
- He or she who exercises his or her profession with professionalism, as above defined, is said to be an outstanding professional.

Professionalization is the collective and individual process of construing a profession and of acquiring professional competence.

---

[7] Justice Potter Stewart, *Jacobellis v. State of Ohio, 378 U.S. 184, 197* (1964) (http://caselaw.lp.findlaw.com/scripts/getcase.pl?court=usandvol=378andinvol=184).

- Collectively, professionalization is the process of an occupation raising its level of professionality. Its main variables are its nature, the progress of its unique knowledge, the dynamism of its actors, the social status of its clients and the political interest involved in it.
- Individually, professionalization is the process of professional learning and socialization, that is, both of the acquisition of knowledge and of internalizing the values, attitudes and manners by means of which the professional in becoming learns a whole professional culture and posture.

Professional competence means the expertise peculiar to the members of a profession. It is specialized and professional in proportion to its levels of abstraction, systematization, applicability and efficiency. In addition, the professions with higher professionality, in particular, possess another dimension, concerned with values, conduct, attitudes, qualities and manners. Professional competence encompasses, therefore, a theoretical, cognitive-practical, ethical and personal content.

Professional Standards are the criterion of professionalism. "Standard" is a term with diverse uses, as John Sayer (2000) observes:

> Etymologically it has to do with both extending and standing. It is sometimes used to mean that to which we aspire, with superlatives attached: the highest standard. At other times it may mean the generally accepted norm, as in standard measurement, or the average. Or yet again, it may be used to mean the lowest acceptable level. Translated into a code of conduct, the first of these might be the values which inform a profession, the second would be norms on which work can be done to change them, and the third would have to do with professional unacceptability. Translated into codified rules of practice, the focus would be the third, where the word 'standards' is uttered with a growl and the point is reached at which unacceptable practice becomes professionally actionable. (p. 164)

Sayer quotes Nigel Harris (1996) who:

> … in his encyclopedic directory of codes of conduct in the UK attempts to distinguish broadly between codes of ethics, codes of conduct and rules of practice, whilst observing that each expression is variously used. Codes of ethics will be the short sets of broad ethical principles; codes of conduct will be more detailed and specific; codes of practice govern the way duties are performed. He observes that relatively few codes distinguish between rules which articulate fundamental moral principles to be observed in any circumstance and rules which set down detail of how duties should be performed in order to ensure consistency of practice. (p. 163)

Every occupation has its standards or "rules of art", even if they are not set in a written form, but the main professions have high and codified Professional Standards defining their scope and services; identifying the knowledge, values and qualities that distinguish the profession and should distinguish its professionals; and stating the responsibilities they assume. They are principally Standards for professional fitness, competence, education, practice and conduct.

Professional self-regulation means, as aforementioned, that a profession is entrusted with self-governing statutory powers, in return for its commitment to its clients' and the general public interests by complying with high Professional Standards. Traditionally, it was a privilege of the so-called liberal professions, that is, professions requiring higher educational qualifications and being practiced in an independent manner, but such criteria are no longer so exclusive and distinctive. In the Anglo-Saxon countries, in particular, many more professions and occupations are self-governing, including the teaching profession. This is an issue to be further elaborated later. Before doing so, however, let us examine teaching as a profession.

References

Beaton, G. (2010). *Why professionalism is still relevant*. The University of Melbourne, Melbourne Law School, Legal studies research papers, No. 445. Retrieved January 2013, from www. professions.com.au/Files/Professionalism_Beaton.pdf

Dingwall, R. (2008). *Essays on professions*. Aldershot: Ashgate.

Dubar, C., & Tripier, P. (2009). *Sociologie des professions*. Paris: Armand Colin (first published in 1998).

Gorman, E., & Sandefur, R. (2011). 'Golden age', quiescence, and revival: How the sociology of professions became the study of knowledge-bases work. *Work and Occupations, 38*(3), 275–302. Retrieved January 2013, from www.virginia.edu/sociology/publications/faculty% 20articles/Gorman-Articles/Gorman-SandefurWandO-Knowledge-BasedWork.pdf

Hamilton, N. (2008). Assessing professionalism: measuring progress in the formation of an ethical professional identity. *University of St. Thomas Law Journal, 5,* 101–143 (Legal studies research paper series, 8–10). http://papers.ssrn.com/sol3/papers.cfm?abstract_id=1118204##

Hughes, E. Ch. (1958). *Men and their work*. Glencoe: The Free Press. https://ia700408.us.archive. org/23/items/mentheirwork00hugh/mentheirwork00hugh.pdf

Ingersoll, R., & Perda, D. (2008). The status of teaching as a profession. In J. Ballantine & J. Spade (Eds.), *Schools and society: A sociological approach to education* (pp. 106–118). Los Angeles: Pine Forge Press.

McRuer, J. Ch. (1968–1971). *Report of the royal commission inquiry into civil rights: Report number one*, (Vol. 3). Toronto: Queens' Printer.

Ramsey, G. (2000). *Quality matters: Revitalising teaching: Critical times, critical choices: Report of the review of teacher education*, New South Wales. www.det.nsw.edu.au/teachrev/reports/ reports.pdf

Reagan, T. (2010). The professional status of teaching. In *The sage handbook of philosophy of education* (Chap. 14). London: Sage Publications.

Sayer, J. (2000). *The general teaching council*. London: Cassell.

Spada. (2009). *British professions today: The state of the sector*. www.ukipg.org.uk/executive_ group_resources/spada-british-professions-today.pdf

Villegas-Reimers, E. (2003). *Teacher professional development: An international review of the literature*. Paris: UNESCO, International Institute for Educational Planning. http://unesdoc. unesco.org/images/0013/001330/133010e.pdf

Chapter 5
Teaching as a Profession

Abstract According to international and national reports and studies, the overall status of the teaching profession is not very prestigious (and indeed far from it), as already mentioned. Underlying its widely degraded status—and being decisive for its future—is the *crux* of grasping its very identity. Teachers should consider themselves and be considered as professionals of the right to education and of pedagogic communication, the centre of gravity of their professionalism being interpersonal relationship. At the core of the teaching profession is its unique and far-reaching ethical dimension. The improvement of its quality should therefore begin at … the beginning. The human quality of the candidates to exercising the profession should be taken into account when deciding on the criteria for entering professional education and evaluating professional performance. Besides selection, education and evaluation, improving the quality of the teaching profession should also include other aspects of its professional and social status, such as working conditions, as well as pay and career perspectives, without overlooking the relevance of school management. The future of the teaching profession is obviously tied to that of the school. Teachers should become professionals of example. Professional exemplarity should be understood as an exceptional incarnation of a blend of qualities, values and knowledge. The teaching profession should be principally responsible for attracting the best human beings. How? by means of outstanding professional self-governing bodies, composed of people holding a passionate and inspiring vision.

Keywords Teaching profession status · Teaching profession identity · Professional ethics · Teaching profession quality · Teaching profession future

Just as improving educational quality demands a systemic, holistic approach, in order to address its varied factors, improving the quality of the teaching profession requires a global approach to its professional and social status. As the Report of the New York 2012 Summit points out: "Countries need to substitute virtuous cycles of raising the status of the profession for the vicious cycles of decline" (Asia Society 2012, p. 15). The European Commission *Document* (2012) observes:

A. Reis Monteiro, *The Teaching Profession*, SpringerBriefs in Education,
DOI 10.1007/978-3-319-12130-7_5

Policy on the teaching professions has in many Member States been a case of incremental, piecemeal changes. [...] But if the teaching professions are to meet the significant challenges, a systemic response is needed with coherent and consistent policies and programmes for their recruitment, selection, initial education, induction, professional development and working conditions. (p. 20)

Below, after synthesizing the status of the teaching profession, a definition of its identity is proposed, the significance of its ethical dimension is highlighted, a conception of its quality is presented, and a vision of its future is submitted.

5.1 Status

As already said, two terms are frequently used with respect to the status of the teaching profession worldwide: *decline* and (lack of) *recognition*. In 1997, the Report of the Joint ILO/UNESCO Committee of Experts[1] drew a landscape of the teaching profession that deserves to be recalled in some length:

18. The Joint Committee observes that, in virtually every country reported upon, the status of teachers in the relative employment hierarchy still remains low or, in some instances, has actually deteriorated in recent years. This recurrent and fundamental theme helps explain the reported decline in morale of teachers. For example, in Africa, many areas of Latin America and some countries of Eastern Europe, teachers receive such poor salaries that they often have to seek other means of survival, including taking second jobs. In some areas the concept of 'privatization' of teaching is tending to produce situations in which fee-paying students receive preferential treatment in contrast to those who are not. With some notable exceptions, teacher remuneration and status compare adversely with those of other professions, with the result that the more able students are not attracted to the teaching profession, or leave it when they find better employment opportunities. The increasing personal insecurity of teachers and violence in schools are phenomena which impact adversely on teacher morale and performance. Additionally, in many industrialised countries teachers have been under fairly consistent public criticism from families, business leaders and politicians alike, as a consequence of an apparent loss of public confidence in teachers and education systems.

19. It is reported that some factors which contribute to the perceived unattractiveness of the teaching profession to the brighter students include:

   – the stress and teacher dissatisfaction associated with the gradual breakdown of traditional consensus regarding the purposes and functions of education and, more specifically, the role of teachers;
   – recruitment restrictions and a loss of attractiveness, provoking a general ageing of the profession, particularly at the school level, which is seen as inhibiting an infusion of new blood, ideas and career progression;
   – the processes of rationalization, which have had an adverse effect on professional status in many countries, where teaching is seen as something of a second class option. This has contributed to the steady feminisation of the profession at the pre-

---

[1] www.ilo.org/wcmsp5/groups/public/—ed_dialogue/—sector/documents/meetingdocument/wcms_162259.pdf.

secondary levels and, therefore, tends to stereotype such areas of teaching as a women's profession with the result that fewer men are attracted to it. Real equality between men and women is often still the exception rather than the rule.

20. Whilst there are variable factors operating within regions, some general causes for a decline in teacher status have been:

   – a perceived failure of Governments to interact effectively with teachers to establish proper educational policies and to provide resources to implement them, especially as public resources directed to education have declined;

   – a neglect by teachers to promote their own status and professionalism in times of economic austerity. Almost by default, they have allowed a community perception to develop that their main preoccupation has been with their own salaries and benefits, which may consume up to 90 % of the education budget in many countries;

   – the emergence of community perceptions that teachers are failing to deliver an educational outcome considered to be satisfactory, thereby attracting widespread public and governmental criticism, to the detriment of their professional status;

   – in the context of government attempts to reduce costs, the efforts by teachers' organisations to resist measures which increase class sizes and reduce teacher qualifications, conditions and pay, have often been characterised as major obstacles to educational development. This dynamic has tended to denigrate teachers and lower the general community perception of the quality and value of public education. Schools and educational professionals are bearing much of the blame for the increasing difficulty of coping with enormous economic and societal changes which have been taking place, including economic globalization, social dislocation, slowly growing economic productivity and increased unemployment.

This landscape has not significantly changed. Drawing on the international and national reports and studies referred to earlier, the overall status of the teaching profession may be summarized as follows:

- *Professional and social status not very prestigious*

   – It is, in general, seen as a profession easily accessible, that is, without demanding selection, education and evaluation criteria.
   – It is not, in general, well-paid, compared with other professions with an analogous academic background.
   – Its autonomy is limited by its unique political dimension.
   – It does not control the main factors of its success.
   – Its practice levels are frequently below the desirable and even the acceptable.
   – It is often ill-treated by reductive, unjust and unmotivating appraisal.
   – It is deprofessionalized when teachers are treated as "craft" and a mere category of public servants.
   – It is highly populated, and the social basis for its recruitment is not high.
   – It is also affected by the fact of being considered mostly a female job.
   – Its most direct "clients" are "minors".
   – It does not generally have stimulating prospects for professional advancement.
   – It is a familiar profession, without the mystery of distance of other more esoteric professions.

- *Deficient or degraded working conditions*

    - Work places frequently not dignified and not welcoming.
    - Overpopulated and highly heterogeneous classes.
    - Increasingly growing and extended programmes.
    - Overloading tasks.
    - Lack of resources.

- *Other aspects of a devaluated public image*

    - The age-old image of the ignorant and pedantic pedagogue persists in literature and arts.
    - There is a generalized presumption of competence regarding education.
    - It is, perhaps, the profession most exposed to the public opinion, such visibility making it more scrutinizable and increasing the social repercussions of the shortcomings and mediocrity of the worst professionals.

- *Other factors*

    - Students' disaffection from school.
    - Accelerated rhythm of school reforms.
    - Aggressiveness of students and sometimes of parents.
    - It is a profession without a strong "conscience of class", so much as it is often a second choice profession, and may be exercised on a part-time basis.
    - The school and the teaching profession have lost their traditional near-monopoly as sources of knowledge.

Other aspects may be pointed out:

- School and teachers are frequently social scapegoats. Three decades ago, a famous American Report began by remarking, referring to schools: "They are routinely called on to provide solutions to personal, social, and political problems that the home and other institutions either will not or cannot resolve" (National Commission on Excellence in Education 1983). MacBeath (2012) notices too: "Teachers, unlike most professions, are burdened with excessive expectations from society at large, caught between high expectation and low professional esteem (Punch and Tuetteman 1996)" (p. 14).
- It is said that teachers do not work very much, have many holidays, often miss days and are not held accountable for what they (do not) do.

    In many countries, there is a generalized perception that teachers work fewer hours than do other professionals. This perception is frequently based on the fact that teachers' working time has been defined historically as only the amount of time spent in the classroom. This definition does not account for the amount of time spent at school but outside the classroom, the time dedicated to professional development, or the time used to plan lessons and grade assignments. In some countries, this misconception about teachers' working time may have decreased their social recognition, which may in turn affect their motivation. (World Bank 2012, p. 12)

- The teaching profession is sometimes targeted by "discourses of derision, of blaming and shaming, among politicians and the media, that have helped create and sustain a loss of public faith in, and regard for, teachers and their work" (Whitty 2006). Following the New York 2011 Summit Report: "In a number of systems, including those of Denmark and Norway, a media climate that berated teachers is believed to have contributed to a decline in the attractiveness and status of the profession" (Asia Society 2011, p. 7).
- In addition: "We are confronted with the paradox that while the nature of learning has been shown to be more determined by influences that lie outside of schools, teachers have become increasingly more accountable for the performance of their pupils" (MacBeath 2012, p. 62).

As a consequence, there are "chronic shortages in many developing countries", and "around half of all countries worldwide are experiencing a teacher gap in relation to meeting Universal Primary Education goals by 2015. Although sub-Saharan Africa suffers the most widespread and chronic shortages, all regions have primary teacher gaps (UNESCO–UIS 2009, 2010)" (ILO 2012, p. 224). Furthermore, several countries "will soon have to replace large numbers of staff who have left the teaching professions or who will retire shortly. The ageing of teachers becomes an alarming trend in many Member States and corresponding policies will need to be balanced against the changes in the school-age population" (European Commission 2012, p. 6). More precisely:

- There are countries without a general lack of teachers, because the profession is prestigious, attractive and competitive, as in Finland. Also in Japan what attracts young people to teaching "is primarily the high regard in which teachers are held. Teaching is a highly desirable job—there are seven applicants for every teaching position in Japan" (OECD 2011b, p. 145).
- There are countries that do not lack teachers, because the school population is diminishing, and because of a lack of better professional alternatives. Portugal is an example: in the spring 2014, a special competition to fill about 2,000 teaching posts received about 40,000 candidates.
- There are countries lacking teachers in some subjects or regions. They are numerous. "Difficulty in recruiting teachers either across the board or in certain subjects or geographic areas is widespread around the globe" (Asia Society 2012, p. 12). For instance:

  Sweden's biggest challenge in teacher quality is the attractiveness of the teaching profession. Too many teachers are unqualified for their jobs, especially in math and science, and the Swedish government believes this is a major reason for Sweden's lower PISA scores. Over time, teaching had become an unattractive profession: In one recent year, only ten people had applied to become chemistry teachers in the whole country, for example. (Asia Society 2013, p. 8)

- There are countries with high professional attrition. For instance, in the USA, in some cities, "up to 50 % of teachers leave teaching within 5 years, while in the United Kingdom the attrition rate is 25 %" (Asia Society 2012, p. 14). The

European Commission *Document* (2012) informs: "As many as 40 % may leave before 5 years in Belgium, and 20 % in the Netherlands" (p. 33). According to the 2013 *MetLife Survey of the American Teacher*[2]:

> Principals' satisfaction with their jobs in the public schools has decreased nine percentage points since it was last measured in 2008. In that same period, teacher satisfaction has dropped precipitously by 23 percentage points, including a five-point decrease in the last year, to the lowest level it has been in the survey in 25 years. A majority of teachers report that they feel under great stress at least several days a week, a significant increase from 1985 when this was last measured. (p. 4)

- There are countries where teachers are lacking because the profession is not prestigious, attractive and competitive. This is the most frequent situation. And when "teaching is not perceived as an attractive profession, and teaching does not change in fundamental ways, there is a risk that the quality of schools will decline and a downward spiral will be difficult to reverse" (OECD 2005, p. 18).

The OECD 2005 study had already warned that, although teachers are the most significant and costly resource in schools, the quality of teaching and learning necessarily declines when school systems "respond to teacher shortages in the short-term by some combination of lowering qualification requirements for entry to the profession; assigning teachers to teach in subject areas in which they are not fully qualified; increasing the number of classes that teachers are allocated; or by increasing class sizes" (p. 9). The risk of a vicious circle is recalled in the New York 2012 Summit Report:

> Some countries also reveal a worrying downward spiral: Teacher shortages lead to lower standards for entry, producing lowered confidence in the profession, resulting in more prescriptions to teachers, which in turn tend to drive the most talented teachers out of the profession. By contrast to this vicious cycle, the highest performing countries have found ways to maintain or continuously raise the quality of teachers and teaching, producing a virtuous cycle. (Asia Society 2012, p. 12)

Summing up: improving the quality of the teaching profession requires a global approach to its professional and social status. It includes seeking to define its very professional identity, highlighting its unique ethical dimension, designing a consistent conception of its quality and an inspiring vision of its future.

5.2 Identity

Underlying the widely degraded status of the teaching profession—and being decisive for its future—is the *crux* of grasping its very identity.

There are two main sociological approaches to professional identity: the attributes approach and the difference approach.

---

[2] www.metlife.com/assets/cao/foundation/MetLife-Teacher-Survey-2012.pdf.

- *Attributes approach*
  The attributes approach consists in comparing an occupation with the attributes of the "professional model". The latter refers, as we saw above, to occupations with high professional and social status, i.e. which are very specialized (knowledge-based), committed to high standards (Professional Ethics, in particular), largely autonomous (individually and collectively), generally well-paid and prestigious.
- *Difference approach*
  The difference approach consists in identifying the characteristics peculiar to an occupation to cultivate them and advocate for the improvement of its professional and social status.

By its very nature, the teaching profession should not aim at fitting into the attributes approach and *mimicking the liberal professions*. It is an epistemic community, i.e. a profession possessing and applying specialized knowledge, but will never have the certainties and guarantees of efficiency comparable to professions with other epistemic bases. The teaching profession is different and should assume and cultivate its differences.

In his Preface to a *White Paper* presented to the UK Parliament, the Secretary of State for Education, after affirming that teachers are "society's most valuable asset", wrote: "There is no calling nobler, no profession more vital and no service more important than teaching. [...] The importance of teaching cannot be over-stated" (Department for Education 2010). It is "perhaps the most important profession of all for good", in the opinion of Charlotte Leslie, member of the Education Committee of the UK Parliament (in Leslie 2013, Foreword, p. 7). It is also claimed that it is the second oldest profession...[3]

Indeed, the teaching profession may be considered as the most universal, fundamental, ethical and personal profession.

- *The most universal* insofar as school assistance is compulsory.
- *The most fundamental* insofar as most professions are learned with teachers.
- *The most ethical* insofar as it is a profession of the learning to be human and to live humanly with other human beings.
- *The most personal* insofar as the core of teachers' professionalism is interpersonal relationship.

The teaching profession is unique, moreover, for other motives: it may be considered as the most democratic, paradoxical and impossible profession as well.

- *The most democratic* because it does not consist only in professionals applying specialized knowledge, but also in sharing their knowledge, by means of the learning they manage to cause.

---

[3] http://plato.stanford.edu/entries/education-philosophy.

- *The most paradoxical* because its accomplishment is great inasmuch it succeeds in becoming unnecessary, i.e. when the disciples no longer need—and can even supersede—the master.
- *The most impossible* because its performance depends, much more than in any other profession, on the will and attitude of its "clients", which are not always the most interested in its services.

The teaching profession distinguishes itself, therefore, by its relational intensity, functional complexity, contextual density, demanding great maturity and reflexivity, capacity for professional spontaneity and a pedagogical *Fingerspitzengefühl* (a "sixth sense" or professional insight). This is highlighted by a study published by the Netherlands' Education Council (2013) that explores "the challenging and complex occupational practice of teachers, and calls for more attention, in debate and policy, to be paid to the personal professionalism needed for teachers' good performance inside and outside the classroom" (p. 7). Personal professionalism is driven by a "practical wisdom" according to the classic distinction made by Aristotle (384–322 BC), in his *Nicomachean Ethics* (1925) between *epistémé* (theoretical knowledge), *techné* (technical competence), and *phronésis* (practical wisdom). Teachers' practical wisdom "does not refer to abstract knowledge that can be generalized or to technically correct performance, but to doing the right thing in the right way in concrete practice situations".

> This personal core of professionalism is constantly developing during a teacher's career. [...] They increasingly recognize the important features of situations better and more quickly, and react more and more adequately to these situations. Practical wisdom plays an important role in the quality of professional performance, but by being implicit and specific to situations it is not easily measurable with the help of standardized, generic instruments. (pp. 31, 32)

In other words, "practical wisdom refers to seeing, hearing, and feeling sharply what is going on in a given situation, and what is the essence of the situation. This 'feeling' for the situation enables teachers to (rapidly) take the right decisions and to act adequately in their occupational practice" (p. 40).

How then should the teaching profession be most properly defined?

It may be said that a profession consists in a *knowing-well-doing something*, that is, in applying an expertise to addressing human needs and problems. Consequently, defining the teaching profession should be, basically, to make clear what distinguishes their professionals from the parents most capable of educating their children, as well as from other professionals holding common academic background.

The scope of the teaching profession being education, defining its identity implies grasping the nature of the educational phenomenon. The following two essential ideas are proposed:

- Education is fundamentally a phenomenon of communication and a kind of power, raising the question of its legitimacy.
- Education possessing the normative statute of "human right", its legitimacy is to be found in the "right to education".

A full justification of these statements is beyond the scope of this study. If they are granted, however, it may be concluded that teachers should consider themselves and be considered as professionals of the right to education and of pedagogic communication, the centre of gravity of their professionalism being interpersonal relationship. This should be understood as follows:

- The right to education is a new right to a new education, i.e. a right of every human being to the education he or she is entitled to, as internationally agreed.
- Pedagogic communication is that whose source of legitimacy and principle of quality is the normative content of the right to education that includes respecting the equal human dignity and all rights of the right-holders.
- The centrality of the interpersonal relationship in education means that the difference and distinction of the teaching profession lie not only in knowing how to teach some subject, but in the significance of the whole influence teachers exert on the development of the personality of every child, adolescent or youth they encounter in their classes.

As a consequence, it may be argued that the *teachers' knowing-well-doing something* should consist in a *knowing-to-be-and-to-communicate-pedagogically*, that is, in their being the persons they should be, knowing who their students are and how they learn and develop, as well as knowing about education both as a human right, with its ethical–legal normative content, and as a process of communication, with its learning contents and forms.

At the core of the teaching profession is, therefore, its unique and far-reaching ethical dimension.

5.3 Ethics

Every professional occupation, both humble and proud, holds an ethical dimension insofar as it implies some trustworthy relationship between persons and some kind of responsibility for what it does. There are hundreds of Professional Ethics texts adopted worldwide.[4] The ethical dimension is more demanding in proportion to the extent to which the profession deals most directly and essentially with the human person; the more powerful as its means are and greater its autonomy is; deeper as the asymmetry between the professionals and their clients is; and broader its public exposure is. Thus is a profession in the densest sociological meaning of the term, whose cognitive and ethical dimensions are, in practice, deeply interwined. As "A Teacher's Professional Ethics and Ethical Principles" reads, adopted by the Trade Union of Education in Finland (OAJ)[5]:

---

[4] See the database of the Center for the Study of Ethics in the Professions (CSEP, created in 1976), Illinois Institute of Technology (USA) (http://ethics.iit.edu/codes/coe.html).

[5] Kindly made electronically available by OAJ (February 2013).

> The sense of responsibility attached to the practising of a profession is based on knowledge and vocational skills on the one hand and on the values and norms that form the foundation of the work on the other. Both are essential, and neither can replace the other. Good ethical principles cannot compensate for poor professional skills, and good professional skills cannot make up for a lack of ethical principles.

A Professional Ethics serves several purposes. It is a normative framework adopted by a profession, at the national or international level, formally and publicly proclaiming its core values, which are the source of the professional responsibilities, laid down in principles and duties (and implying rights too). It may be a mere declaration, aspirational in nature, having a simply moral value, or it may be a legally enforceable code, with a structure and content more or less elaborated. It may begin with a statement of its philosophic underpinnings, including the purpose of education as a human right and its importance to democracy and development. For example, in the Canadian Code of Ethics for Psychologists[6]:

> Four ethical principles, to be considered and balanced in ethical decision making, are presented. Each principle is followed by a statement of those values that are included in and give definition to the principle. Each values statement is followed by a list of ethical standards that illustrate the application of the specific principle and values to the activities of psychologists. The standards range from minimal behavioural expectations […] to more idealized, but achievable, attitudinal and behavioural expectations. In the margin, to the left of the standards, key words are placed to guide the reader through the standards and to illustrate the relationship of the specific standards to the values statement.

No written Professional Ethics comprehends all possible situations, however, as the McRuer Report (1968–1971) notes:

> It may be impossible to stipulate in advance all the varieties and shades of activity which will be regarded as professional misconduct, and a general clause providing for discipline for 'professional misconduct' will always be necessary so as to allow the profession to take account of unforeseen types of misbehaviour. The presence of such a general provision does not make it any less desirable that each body exercising disciplinary powers of self-government should have a code of ethics. (pp. 1190, 1191)

Therefore, there are no "cookbook" recipes; personal judgment and decision are always required. As the Software Engineering Code of Ethics and Professional Practice—Association for Computing Machinery, Inc. and the Institute for Electrical and Electronics Engineers, Inc (USA)[7] cautions: "The Code is not a simple ethical algorithm that generates ethical decisions". The Code of Ethics of the National Association of Social Workers (NASW, USA)[8] notes: "The Code offers a set of values, principles, and standards to guide decision making and conduct when

---

[6] www.cpa.ca/cpasite/userfiles/Documents/Canadian%20Code%20of%20Ethics%20for%20Psycho.pdf.

[7] www.acm.org/serving/se/code.htm#full.

[8] www.socialworkers.org/pubs/code/code.asp.

ethical issues arise. It does not provide a set of rules that prescribe how social workers should act in all situations".

At present, professional ethical standards are largely internationalized for these main reasons: the universalization of the principle of respect for human rights, the globalisation of the world and the international organization of professions.[9] Human rights, in particular, are a fundamental ethical source. For example, the aforementioned OAJ Professional Ethics states: "One major point of departure for the ethical principles set out here has been the UN's Universal Declaration of Human Rights". The Code of Ethics and Professional Conduct of the Association for Computing Machinery (USA)[10] refers to "an obligation to protect fundamental human rights and to respect the diversity of all cultures" (1.1).

Another normative source is Compared Professional Ethics, that is, the ethical standards of the same and of other professions at national and international level. For example, the Canadian Code of Ethics for Psychologists[11] informs in its pre-amble: "In addition to the responses provided by Canadian Psychologists, the values statements and ethical standards have been derived from interdisciplinary and international ethics codes, provincial and speciality codes of conduct, and ethics literature".

"Code of Ethics", "Code of Conduct", "Code of Practice"—are expressions sometimes used interchangeably. Following an ILO *Handbook* (2012), referring to the teaching profession, they may be distinguished as follows:

- A code of ethics is generally a short document with a set of ethical principles, usually limited to broad and general fundamental values that are meant to guide the teacher in their everyday practice [...].
- A code of conduct is more detailed and addresses specific situations as well as actions to be taken or not. Codes of conduct are often broad, apply to the overall conduct and behaviour of the teacher and are likely to be more effective if they include specific sanctions to be taken if a teacher breaches the code.
- A code of practice contains ethical standards, as well as rules of professional duties. Codes of practice are often designed and implemented by professional bodies and they are concerned mostly with what kind of teaching happens in the classroom, as opposed to the overall conduct of the teacher. (p. 98)

In any case: "A code of conduct or practice should include some general statements of principles related to commonly agreed ethical principles of good teaching practice and behaviour" (p. 99). Furthermore: "To be relevant, a good code of conduct should be rooted in real problems and sources of unethical behaviours by teachers" (p. 100), which implies teachers' participation in its development. "Real involvement takes time, resources and commitment, but failure to integrate fully teachers' views will seriously undermine the credibility and effectiveness of a code of conduct or practice" (p. 101).

---

[9] The European Federation of Psychologists' Associations refers to its Code of Ethics as a "Meta-Code" (www.efpa.be/ethics.php).

[10] www.acm.org/constitution/code.html.

[11] www.cpa.ca/publications.

Turning to the education field, it has no tradition of Professional Ethics. The main explanation for this absence is likely the fact that the most teachers are public servants governed by Boards, Departments, and Ministries of Education. The ethical dimension of the education professions is also, in general, undervalued by their associations. It is understandable that it not be a priority when other priorities are urgent, but it might also be asked: Is there a higher priority for a profession than its public credibility and honour?

The paramount importance of the teaching profession adopting ethical standards is already highlighted in the ILO/UNESCO Recommendation concerning the Status of Teachers (1966)[12] that states:

> 70. Recognizing that the status of their profession depends to a considerable extent upon teachers themselves, all teachers should seek to achieve the highest possible standards in all their professional work. [...]
> 73. Codes of ethics or of conduct should be established by the teachers' organizations, since such codes greatly contribute to ensuring the prestige of the profession and the exercise of professional duties in accordance with agreed principles.

The UNESCO Recommendation concerning the Status of Higher Education Teaching Personnel (1997)[13]—that, along with the ILO/UNESCO 1966 Recommendation, forms the main international legal framework for the teaching profession—encompasses similar provisions.

The interest for the ethical dimension of the teaching profession increased in the 1990s and 2000s. Elizabeth Campbell (2008) indicates the year 1990 as a turning point in the research concerning the subject, mentioning studies such as *The Moral Dimensions of Teaching* (Goodlad et al. 1990), *The Moral Base for Teacher Professionalism* (Sockett 1993), and "Teaching as a Moral Activity" (David Hansen, in *Handbook of Research on Teaching*, 2001). The terminology of the writings and texts on Professional Ethics in education is varied. Here are some examples:

- In English: *Professional Ethics in Education, Applied Ethics for Educators, Ethics for Teachers, Ethics of Teaching.*
- In French: *Éthique éducative, Déontologie de l'éducateur, Déontologie du métier d'enseignant, Éthique et déontologie dans les métiers de l'éducation.*
- In Italian: *Deontologia della professionalità educativa, Deontologia pedagogica, Ética professionale degli insegnanti, Deontologia professionale degli insegnanti.*
- In German: *Pädagogishe Ethik, Ethik für Pädagogen, Ethik des Erziehers.*
- In Spanish: *Deontología de la educación, Deontología de las profesiones educativas, Deontología educativa, Deontología pedagógica, Deontología del profesor, Ética docente, Ética y deontología docente, Código de ética del profesional de la docencia.*

---

[12] http://portal.unesco.org/en/ev.php-URL_ID=13084andURL_DO=DO_TOPICandURL_SECTION =201.html.

[13] http://portal.unesco.org/en/ev.php-URL_ID=13144andURL_DO=DO_TOPICandURL_SECTION =201.html.

- In Portuguese: *Ética deontológica, Deontologia pedagógica, Ética e deontologia dos professores, Ética e deontologia docente, Código deontológico dos professores, Deontologia da profissão docente, Deontologia das profissões da educação.*

A significant expression of the interest for the ethical dimension of the education professions was the adoption by Education International (EI) of a Declaration on Professional Ethics in 2001.[14] It invokes the 1966 ILO/UNESCO Recommendation, the 1997 UNESCO Recommendation, and the United Nations Convention on the Rights of the Child (1989) as well[15] (which are often referred to in texts on Professional Ethics in the education field). The preamble of the EI Declaration states:

> 5. The teaching profession may benefit greatly from a discussion about the core values of the profession. Such raising of consciousness about the norms and ethics of the profession may contribute to increasing job satisfaction among teachers and education personnel, to enhancing their status and self-esteem, and to increasing respect for the profession in society.

Another expression of the increasing importance recognized to Professional Ethics in education is the Project on Teacher Codes of Conduct launched by the UNESCO International Institute for Educational Planning (IIEP), as part of its Medium Term Plan (2008–2013), following a research project on "Ethics and corruption in education" launched in 2001.[16] It included an "e-Forum on Teacher Codes of Conduct" that took place from November 21 to December 2, 2011, with the participation of about 900 representatives of diverse education sectors and levels of responsibility worldwide, including Ministries of Education and Non-Governmental Organizations (NGOs). The final Report reads[17]:

> As indicated in the literature concerning teachers codes of conduct (Van Nuland 2009), the main purposes of codes can include a variety of objectives: providing guidelines through ethical rules, holding teachers responsible and accountable for their actions, protection of clients (in this case, children), enhancing the professional status of the teaching profession, and creating and maintaining professional identity. […]
> Drawing in the e-forum participants' stated experiences in their respective countries, the following major difficulties encountered in the enforcement of a code of conduct for teachers were mentioned:
>
> – a top to bottom approach;
> – imposition of the code rather than adherence to it;
> – a lack of knowledge of the code among teachers;
> – no inclusion of the code in teacher training;
> – outdated codes that need to be revised;
> – weak supervisory structures;

---

[14] www.ei-ie.org/en/websections/content_detail/3270.

[15] EI is a world Federation of about 400 professional organizations in the education field, representative of about 30 million professionals in more than 170 countries and territories. www.ei-ie.org/worldcongress/docs/WC04Res_DeclarationProfEthics_e.pdf.

[16] Teachercodes.iiep.unesco.org/index.php?lang = EN.

[17] www.iiep.unesco.org/fileadmin/user_upload/Cap_Dev_Training/Virtual_Institute/pdf/Forums/IIEP-UNESCO_Forum_Teacher_Codes_Report.pdf.

- political interference;
- the role of teacher unions to protect teachers rather than to discipline them;
- the situational difficulties encountered by teachers such as low pay and a large number of pupils;
- corruption and nepotism; and
- different cultural backgrounds.

What is at stake in education is too human to be left to teachers' moral subjectivity and relativity, especially because the teaching profession is one of the most exposed to public scrutiny. Teachers work in a kind of goldfish bowl, in daily contact with dozens of children or adolescents, through whom their behaviour resounds in families and society. If their competence and conduct are not professionally acceptable, the profession's public image is significantly and negatively affected.

As a consequence, if no learned profession should limit its professional ideal to its scientific-technical, functional and instrumental dimension, neglecting other human dimensions, much less should the education professions do so, which hold a deep ethical dimension.[18] The education professions may be considered as the most ethical ones (see Campbell 2008), principally when their "clients" are children and adolescents who are vulnerable human beings and subject to compulsory schooling. They are the most ethical professions to the extent that education may be considered as the most ethical professional field, for reasons that may be summarized as follows:

- The human being is essentially educable and moral.
- Education may be considered as the greatest human power and responsibility.
- The pedagogical relation is, perhaps, the most asymmetrical professional relation, especially when children are involved.
- Education professionals are for children and adolescents, beyond parents, the most significant other persons, that is, their most influential human references.

In this respect, the Supporting Statement of the National Board for Professional Teaching Standards (NBPTS, USA) affirms[19]:

> The ethical dimensions of teaching also distinguish it from other professions. Unique demands arise because the client's attendance is compulsory and, more importantly,

---

[18] The philosopher Olivier Reboul (1925–1992) said that "every teacher is a teacher of Morals, even without his or her knowing" (1971, p. 109).

[19] www.nbpts.org/UserFiles/File/what_teachers.pdf
The NBPTS webpage reads:

National Board for Professional Teaching Standards, known simply as National Board, is an independent, nonprofit organization. It was formed in 1987 to advance the quality of teaching and learning by developing professional standards for accomplished teaching, creating a voluntary system to certify teachers who meet those standards and integrating board-certified teachers into educational reform efforts. (See more at: http://www.nbpts.org/who-we-are#sthash.EMoRVWn1.dpuf)

Other organizations for voluntary certification, at federal level, include the American Board for Certification of Teacher Excellence (ABCTE), the National Center for Alternative Certification (NCAC) and the National Council for Accreditation of Teacher Education (NCATE).

because the clients are children. Thus, elementary, middle and high school teachers are obligated to meet a stringent ethical standard. Other ethical demands derive from the teacher's role as a model of an educated person. Teaching is a public activity; a teacher works daily in the gaze of his or her students, and the extended nature of their lives together in schools places special obligations on the teachers' behavior. Students learn early to read and draw lessons from their teachers' characters. Teachers, consequently, must conduct themselves in a manner students might emulate. Their failure to practice what they preach does not long elude students, parents or peers. Practicing with this additional dimension in mind calls for a special alertness to the consequences of manner and behavior. Standards for professional teaching ought, therefore, to emphasize its ethical nature.

According to the ILO *Handbook* (2012):

A teacher code of conduct has many benefits:

- It can support and protect teachers by outlining clear guidelines and rules of behaviour, serve as a reference point when ethical dilemmas arise and prevent unfair accusations against teachers.
- It can protect parents and pupils against unethical behaviour by teachers and provide rules and procedures for complaints.
- It can promote accountability of schools and teachers to pupils, parents and the community.
- It can enhance teacher professionalism and commitment by holding them to high standards of ethics and increasing their ownership and responsibility over their behaviour and teaching practice. (p. 98)

Indeed:

- Professional Ethics protects the rights and interests of a profession's clients but also the professionals themselves against illegitimate pressure and unfair competition, as well as the profession against its less honest members.
- Professional Ethics reinforces the sentiment of belonging to a profession as a community of shared knowledge and values, thus contributing to a greater awareness of its identity and to its unity.
- Professional Ethics expresses the essence of a profession's culture. It is the core of professionalism. A high ethical profile affirms the identity and magnifies the dignity, honour and prestige of a profession.

After the proclamation of a Professional Ethics, its cultivation must begin by introducing it into professional education. Not as a mere diffuse "cross responsibility" left to the empirical subjectivity and relativity of each teacher educator, condemning it to a purgatory irrelevance, but as an autonomous field of study. Learning a Professional Ethics should mean developing the capacity for thinking, deciding, acting and reacting professionally, that is, responsibly, in accordance with the core values of the profession. In addition, so that it not merely be a series of moralistic exhortations, a mere litany of "do"s and "don't"s without consequences, its breach should be sanctioned by a recognized competent professional body. It would also be highly symbolic to conclude professional education with a solemn and public oath, declaring knowledge of the Professional Ethics and pledging commitment to it.

Professional Ethics should be, therefore, an axial element of the quality of the teaching profession.

5.4 Quality

The 2013 International Summit on the Teaching Profession, in Amsterdam, was dedicated to "Teacher Quality".

> What makes a good teacher, and who gets to decide? This question produced heated debate at the Summit. Agreement on what constitutes a high-quality teacher has to be the starting point for any teacher-appraisal system. In most, but not all countries, these questions are being answered in teacher standards or in other kinds of documents that spell out the responsibilities of the profession. (Asia Society 2013, p. 8)

As Gregor Ramsey (2000) remarked in an Australian Report: "Standards are a more recent mechanism by which the majority of professions give meaning to their professionalism" (p. 125). The adoption of "professional teaching and ethical standards setting out the expected knowledge, skills, attitudes and values of teachers have widespread support within the community and within the profession" (p. 146). In effect:

> Teachers are restricted in their capacity to respond to the debates surrounding societal expectations as they have no framework of standards from within which they can demonstrate the quality of their professional practice. In too many instances they become the punching bag for populist but often ill-informed views which gain credibility because they largely go unchallenged.
> The professional associations, irrespective of any commitments they may have made over the past decade to their desirability, have failed to achieve what is integral to any profession: the development of well-defined and applied standards. (pp. 32, 33)

As already said, Professional Standards are principally standards for professional fitness, competence, education, practice and conduct. They should form the normative framework essential for accreditation of initial and continuing education, for registration and certification, for any possible disciplinary sanction, as well as for the periodic evaluation of performance.

The Standards for the Education, Competence and Professional Conduct of Educators in British Columbia[20] read:

> Standards are a way of communicating to certificate holders and the public the description of the work of educators – what they know, what they are able to do, and how they comport themselves as they serve the public. The Standards provide the foundation and stability on which educators can grow, articulating both the values and characteristics that distinguish the work of educators.

According to the European Commission *Document* (2012), Professional Standards represent an "overall consensus on what teaching and education are for" (p. 28), including "a shared understanding of the competences and qualities that teaching staff require to start, and progress, within the profession" (p. 60).

---

[20] www.bcteacherregulation.ca/documents/AboutUs/Standards/edu_stds.pdf.

In order to encourage the ongoing development of professional competence, such frameworks could define different levels of competence – for example one level for newly
qualified staff, another for experienced teaching staff, and others for staff with specific
responsibilities. Moreover, teacher competence frameworks should take into account the
specificities of each branch of the teaching professions. […]
Such frameworks can have multiple uses: as a tool for self-reflection by student teachers, as
a resource in Teacher Education, as a guide to help teachers identify their personal priorities
for professional learning, as a starting point for school development activities, and as a
guide in recruitment and selection procedures.
So the description of the competences required by teaching staff is, in itself, only useful if it
is embedded in a wider systemic strategy to select the right candidates, develop their core
competences in Initial Teacher Education, and ensure they further develop them throughout
their careers […]. (pp. 27, 28)

Consequently:

It is critical to move from the old bureaucratic conception of teaching, which many current
appraisal systems reflect, in which administrators tell teachers what to do and monitor how
they do it, to a more professional one. The teaching profession needs to own its own
standards in the way that other professions do. (Asia Society 2013, p. 10)

The following addresses the selection of teachers and their education and evaluation, but also other aspects of their professional and social status influencing their
quality, such as working conditions, pay and career perspectives, without overlooking the relevance of school management.

• Selection

Lee Shulman (2005) observed that "professionals not only have to understand and
perform, they have to be certain kinds of human beings". As the teaching profession
is concerned, first and foremost, students *learn their teachers*. Personal qualities are
what mostly make teachers remaining in the affective memory of many children,
adolescents and youth.
According to a New Zealand study:

It is interesting to note that all key groups construe effective teachers in terms of predominantly affective attributes related to interacting with students. According to them,
effective teachers enjoy their work, establish caring relationships with children and are
trusted and respected by parents. Expertise in facilitating student learning […] is rated as
the fifth most important attribute by teachers and principals and the sixth most important by
student teachers. […]
There is a strong sense also that good teachers have an interesting life beyond teaching and
school. (Kane and Mallon 2006, pp. 25, 27)

Because of that, improving the quality of the teaching profession should begin at
… the beginning. The human quality of the candidates exercising the profession
should be taken into account when deciding on the criteria for entering professional

education, as the Ontario's Royal Commission on Learning (1995)[21] clear-cut recommended:

> As we have already noted, the issue of admission to faculties of education is a thorny one, primarily because faculties of education operate as the first gatekeepers to teaching. Concerns focus on two factors: first, there is a belief that admission is too dependent on academic background, specifically undergraduate grades, rather than on personal qualities; second, there is the fact that too few candidates from minority groups are admitted.
> [...]
> Many people believe that personal qualities of character should be the most important criteria for admission to teaching. We agree in principle: the difficulty is that these personal qualities, which are not easily influenced by training, are notoriously difficult to assess in the admissions process.
> [...]
> However, because we agree that personal qualities are critical, we suggest that selection be seen as a process rather than as an event. Faculties can make initial judgments based on academic criteria and experience (plus the way the candidate reflects in writing on that experience), but may not be able to make adequate appraisals of personal qualities until the candidate is in the program. At that time, however, judgments can and should be made.
> Faculty members and associate teachers in schools have been hesitant to exercise their authority as gatekeepers to the profession, apparently being more comfortable with supporting rather than evaluating student teachers. [...]
> Judgments about suitability should be based on clear understandings about teachers and teaching, and should be acknowledged as a responsibility to be shared by faculty and by the schools where student teachers do their field work. We recognize that both faculty members and teachers find it difficult to make such judgments when student teachers are proving unsuitable. We believe, however, that it is crucial for them to recognize their obligation to future generations of elementary and secondary school students. (pp. 294, 295)

Following the OECD (2005) study: "A point of agreement among the various studies is that there are many important aspects of teacher quality that are not captured by the commonly used indicators such as qualifications, experience and tests of academic ability" (p. 27). Furthermore, some researchers "have cautioned that subject matter knowledge might be important up to some level of basic competence but less important thereafter (Ferguson and Womack 1993; Goldhaber and Brewer 2000; Monk and King 1994)" (World Bank 2012, pp. 1, 25). Consequently: "Whilst strong subject knowledge is vital, particularly at secondary level, greater effort is needed to identify which additional personal qualities make candidates well-suited to teaching" (House of Commons 2012, p. 3). They are the most delicate, uncomfortable and neglected dimension of teaching professionalism, but the 1966 ILO/UNESCO Recommendation concerning the Status of Teachers[22] stated long ago:

---

[21] The Royal Commission on Learning was established by the Province of Ontario, in May 1993, "to present a vision and action plan to guide Ontario's reform of elementary and secondary education" for ensuring "that Ontario youth are well prepared for the challenges of the twenty-first century" (Order in Council). The Commission released its report, entitled *For the Love of Learning*, in January 1995.

[22] http://portal.unesco.org/en/ev.php-URL_ID=13084andURL_DO=DO_TOPICandURL_SECTION=201.html.

4. It should be recognized that advance in education depends largely on the qualifications and ability of the teaching staff in general and on the human, pedagogical and technical qualities of the individual teachers. [...]
11. Policy governing entry into preparation for teaching should rest on the need to provide society with an adequate supply of teachers who possess the necessary moral, intellectual and physical qualities and who have the required professional knowledge and skills.

In Finland, for example, access to the profession is very selective. Besides excellent grades, applicants to professional education should have personal, relational and communicational qualities. The selection proceedings include two phases:

- First phase
  The selection's basis is the National Matriculation Examination certification (at the end of the upper secondary school) and other extra-school relevant data.
- Second phase

  - A written exam concerning the contents of some pedagogical books.
  - A school-related activity during which interaction and communication abilities are observed.
  - An interview on the applicant's motivation to enter the profession.

In this regard, an OECD Report (2011a) notes: "Teacher candidates are selected, in part, according to their capacity to convey their belief in the core mission of public education in Finland, which is deeply humanistic as well as civic and economic. The preparation they receive is designed to build a powerful sense of individual responsibility for the learning and well-being of all the students in their care" (p. 11).

In short: "Teaching competences are thus complex combinations of knowledge, skills, understanding, values and attitudes, leading to effective action in situation. Since teaching is much more than a task, and involves values or assumptions concerning education, learning and society, the concept of teacher competences is likely to resonate differently in different national contexts" (European Commission 2012, p. 23). Consequently: "Effective recruitment systems must be based on a clear profile or framework of competences along with appropriate quality assurance measures. These are essential pre-conditions for reengineering recruitment systems, so that they attract and select only the best candidates into initial teacher education (ITE)", that is, "people with the right knowledge, skills, values and attitudes" (29).

• Education

Teachers' professional education is a major challenge for changing their professional and social status. The World Bank *Framework* (2012) recalls:

Possible models of initial teacher education may be classified into three categories. The *concurrent model* is one in which an individual makes the decision to become a teacher at the time of applying to an education program; subject knowledge and pedagogic skills are taught relatively simultaneously. The *consecutive model* is one in which an individual does not need to make the decision to become a teacher at the time of applying to an education program; subject knowledge is taught first, usually leading to a tertiary education degree in a subject and/or discipline, with the option to continue studying to acquire pedagogic skills and become a teacher. *Alternative models*, which include those that do not fit into the concurrent or consecutive models, seek to attract talented individuals (usually professionals) into teaching. These models typically entail a shorter period of teacher-specific education and training, during which individuals develop the qualifications required to become a teacher. (p. 10)

The conception of the teaching profession's education should address, in addition to a wide theoretical vision of the education phenomenon:

- everything the profession does,
- the whole knowledge it requires,
- the fundamental values it should respect,
- the qualities its professionals should cultivate,
- the responsibilities they should be able to assume, individually and collectively.

As a consequence, the teaching profession's education is not just a matter of a *knowledge-base* strictly concerned with what teachers *are expected to know (instruction) and be able to do (didactic)*. Account also should be taken of *how they should be and behave*, not only *to do things right* but principally *to do the right things*. In other words, teachers' professional education should have four main dimensions: theoretical, cognitive-didactic, ethical and personal.

The European Commission *Document* (2012) remarks: "Teaching professionals now face unprecedented challenges; the demands that society places on them are constantly evolving at the same time as our understanding of what makes for effective learning. A key challenge is not so much updating staff subject knowledge, as deepening their understanding of pedagogy and how it connects with the wider world of learning". In fact:

> Our evolving understanding of learning and teaching also includes significant developments in neuroscience and a better and deeper knowledge of the many and varied ways in which people learn. The changes in how we understand learning, and the roles of learner and teacher mean that we can no longer afford to build education systems on the outdated notion that the teacher merely 'transmits' existing knowledge into the heads of passive learners. But nor does the evidence support a complete reliance on 'constructivist' approaches, seeing teachers only as 'co-creating' knowledge with their students. (p. 19)

Educational neuroscience—defined as "a branch of neuroscience that deals with educationally relevant capacities in the brain" (Immordino-Yang and Fischer 2010, p. 2)—found that:

- Thinking and learning are cultural, social, intellectual, moral and emotional processes that consist in constructing neural networks connecting many areas of brain.
- Emotion is "the rudder for learning" (Immordino-Yang 2009, p. 19) and may play a vital role in the cultural and social influences that shape learning, thought and behaviour, as well as in transferring and applying knowledge learned in school to life's situations.
- The main purpose of education should be to cultivate human creativity, that is, the ability to recognize the complexity of situations and to respond in increasingly refined ways.

- As a consequence, "we can no longer justify learning theories that dissociate the mind from the body, the self from social context. [...] In conclusion, there is a revolution imminent in education" (Immordino-Yang 2011, pp. 101, 102).

The findings of educational neuroscience support classical insights of the great authors of the History of Education, confirm what the most competent, conscious and caring educators know from experience, and make evident how wrong, sterile and even harmful the prevailing educational politics are.

Although the teaching profession's education is sometimes criticized for being too theoretical, the truth is that it is never theoretical enough. "There is nothing quite as practical as a good theory", Kurt Lewin (1890–1947) wrote.[23] What matters is that the theory never loses sight of practice. That is why teachers' professional education must have a professionalizing orientation taking place in schools. As a French Report put it: "Initial teaching education should walk with two legs: academic and pedagogical. Its professionalizing vocation should be affirmed" (Dulot et al. 2012, p. 46). The aforementioned House of Commons Report (2012) reads: "It is clear that school-based training is vital in preparing a teacher for their future career, and should continue to form a significant part of any training programme", but not at the expense of the universities' role. "The evidence has left us in little doubt that partnership between schools and universities is likely to provide the highest-quality initial teacher education, the content of which will involve significant school experience but include theoretical and research elements as well" (p. 51).

Another moment of the teaching profession education is induction/probation in schools, after coming to the end of the initial education and before the new teacher assumes his or her professional independence. Nevertheless, its added value depends upon the quality of the teachers taking such a responsibility, which should be experienced and hold a specific preparation. The European Commission *Document* (2012) recommends:

> All beginning teachers should be active in a systematic programme of personal and professional support ('induction') covering their first, crucial years of service; the development of effective induction policy measures should involve all key actors (beginning teaching staff, school leaders, staff and mentors in practice schools, teacher educators, trade unions, policy makers and so on).
>
> Induction can help in tackling the teacher retention issue in several countries, where young (and expensively-trained) teaching staff leaves the profession after only a few years. [...] Moreover, induction programmes can add value by improving the overall quality of teaching, and supporting the development of teacher professionalism.
>
> Ministers have agreed to introduce systematic support for beginning teaching staff; to date, however, [...] only half of European countries or regions offer comprehensive, system-wide support (induction) to professionals after their entering teaching. (p. 33)[24]

---

[23] Lewin, K. (1951). *Field theory in social science: Selected theoretical papers by Kurt Lewin*. New York: Harper and Row.

[24] The Ontario's New Teacher Induction Program (NTIP) is a good example.

Moreover:

> Finally, national induction programmes should be seen as the first part of career-long
> system of continuous professional development. [...]
> Teacher learning should be part of the overall school development plan and be seen as an
> integral part of teacher's regular professional activities. (p. 62)

A career-long global and consistent process of professional development may
include:

> ... a National Teacher Sabbatical Scholarship scheme to allow outstanding teachers to
> undertake education related research, teach in a different school, refresh themselves in their
> subjects, or work in an educational organisation or Government department. In addition to
> the likely positive impacts on individual teachers and schools, we believe such an
> investment would help raise the profession's status amongst existing and potential teachers.
> (House of Commons 2012, p. 52)

Last but not least:

> Teacher educators are crucial for the quality of the teaching workforce, and too often
> neglected in policy-making. [...] The issue of teacher educators' professional competences
> is of paramount importance: if teachers are the most important in-school factor influencing
> the quality of students' learning, the competences of those who educate and support
> teachers must be of the highest order. (European Commission 2012, pp. 52, 54)

Nevertheless, the ILO *Handbook* (2012) notices: "Policies to support the education
of teachers are rarely systematic. [...] Very few Member States have standards
regarding the necessary competences required to be a teacher educator. [...] Policy
on teacher education is fragmented, incomplete and more often than not simply
non-existent" (pp. 13, 225).

In sum:

> Teacher development has three interrelated stages. The first is initial teacher training (ITT),
> geared towards those who have chosen teaching as a career. The second and perhaps most
> neglected aspect of professional development is the induction period, when the newly
> qualified teacher (NQT) begins to teach and, in many countries, undergoes a period of
> supervised mentoring and support, prior to being licensed as a teacher. The third stage is
> continuing professional development (CPD), often provided via in-service education and
> training (INSET), that should be available throughout a teaching career. (p. 223)

Finland comes again as example. There, since the 1970s, all the teaching profession's education programmes are free and take place at university level. Only eight
universities deliver teachers' education courses, in a Department of Education or
beginning in a Department of Humanities or Sciences. At present, all teachers of
basic and secondary schools get a Licence and a Master's (the latter not being
required for kindergarten and preschool professionals).[25] The Master's main area
may be education (for class teachers) or a discipline (for subject teachers).

---

[25] They are organized according to the rules of the European Higher Education Area (EHEA),
created by the Bologna Process, and the European Credit Transfer and Accumulation System (ECTS,
each one corresponding to 25–30 h of learning work, and each academic year consisting of 60 ECTS).

Accordingly, the teaching profession's education takes at least 5 years: 3 years (180 ECTS) for Licence, and two more years (120 ECTS) for a Master's. There is no common syllabus for professional education, but the programmes are coordinated at the national level (with local adjustments). Following Sahlberg (2010):

> Finland's commitment to research-based teacher education means that educational theories, research methodologies and practice all play an important part in preparation programs. [...] Each student thereby builds an understanding of the systemic, interdisciplinary nature of educational practice. Finnish students also learn the skills of how to design, conduct, and present original research on practical or theoretical aspects of education. Another important element of Finnish research-based teacher education is practical training in schools, which is a key component of the curriculum, integrated with research and theory. (p. 4)

In effect, in Finland professional education addresses all the profession's dimensions: personal, ethical, intellectual, civic and practical, including research and creative abilities, preparation to deal with students having special needs and to design and implement learning assessment. Practical education includes:

- Seminars and classes with small groups, in front of colleagues, in the Education Department.
- Supervised practice in schools associated with universities or others with selected professionals.

Teachers educators should be experienced in school teaching, hold research doctorates and apply principles the future teachers should emulate. Therefore:

> No single thing can explain Finland's outstanding educational performance. However, most analysts observe that excellent teachers play a critical role. Among the successful practices that we can take from Finland are:
>
> - The development of rigorous, research based teacher education programs that prepare teachers in content, pedagogy, and educational theory, as well as the capacity to do their own research, and that include field work mentored by expert veterans;
> - Significant financial support for teacher education, professional development, reasonable and equitable salaries, and supportive working conditions;
> - The creation of a respected profession in which teachers have considerable authority and autonomy, including responsibility for curriculum design and student assessment, which engages them in the ongoing analysis and refinement of practice. (p. 8)

Singapore is often referred to as a model of a system of professional development. "Singaporean teachers have about 20 h a week built into their schedule for shared planning and learning, including visits to one another's classrooms, as well as 100 h per year of state-supported professional development outside of their school time" (Darling-Hammond and Rothman 2011, p. 7). In addition, they are given an annual grant to spend, for example, on subscribing to revues or buying informatic material. In Europe:

> Continuing professional development (CPD) is considered as a professional duty for teachers in 24 European countries or regions. In France, Lithuania, Romania and Slovenia, taking part in CPD is a prerequisite for career advancement and salary increases. Ten countries provide teachers with financial allowances for obtaining further CPD qualifications. (European Commission 2012, p. 236)

• Working Conditions

While an education system cannot exceed the quality of its teachers, "equally, the quality of teachers cannot exceed the quality of the system", as the New York 2011 Summit Report highlighted (Asia Society 2011, p. 6). Teachers well-prepared and motivated may be hindered by poor, degraded and undignified working conditions that worsen the difficulties of practicing the profession, and even cause a lack of appeal.

Good working conditions are, first of all, schools that, due to their site, architecture and beauty, convey a message of respect for the children, adolescents and youth going there, and of the great value of what they do there. Eriika Johansson (2011) writes: "School architecture is inescapably influenced by the educational philosophies prevailing at any given period in history" (p. 8). For instance, Sirkkaliisa Jetsonen (2011) remarks: "Pupils seated in orderly rows listening attentively to the teacher, who sits lecturing from a desk on a raised platform in front of the blackboard: this was the authoritarian didactic setting of the traditional classroom" (p. 73). That is a school whose class door is closed for the world when the teaching authority ascends the throne. "Schools were viewed as something akin to adult establishments such as offices, factories or hospitals, or disciplinary and custodial institutions such as army barracks, mental hospitals or prisons" (Nuikkinen 2011, p. 11).

Schools should be architecturally designed for well-being, flexibility and durability, with open, transparent, multifunctional spaces, and others that are private for solitary confinement, autonomous work or in small groups. "A school should be a place that is physically, psychologically and socially safe, promoting the child's growth, health and learning as well as their positive interaction with teachers and fellow pupils. [...] An inspiring, aesthetically pleasing environment enhances the well-being of all who use it" (Johansson 2011, pp. 8, 9). Diane Ravitch (2012) felt, in Finland, "how delightful [it is] to discover a nation that cares passionately about the physical environment in which children learn and adults work", with schools "carefully designed to address the academic, social, emotional, and physical needs of children, beginning at an early age", in beautiful buildings, where quiet children learn with highly educated and caring teachers.

• Pay

A profession's pay level is "a signal of status" (Pearson 2012, p. 25). Consequently, not surprisingly: "A large literature suggests that teacher compensation is an important determinant of whether an individual chooses to go into teaching as a profession" (World Bank 2012, p. 14). In reality: "While paying teachers well is only part of the equation, higher salaries can help school systems to attract the best candidates to the teaching profession. PISA results show that high-performing countries tend to pay teachers higher salaries relative to their per capita gross domestic product (GDP)" (OECD 2014, p. 102).

Although it is not the principal motivation of most candidates for the teaching profession—nor does the research proves a relevant correlation between its pay and the students' outcomes—the fact is that the teaching profession's pay is, in general, inferior to the average of comparable professions. Following the 1998 UNESCO Report: "Even in countries which in recent years have experienced rapid economic growth and increasing prosperity, the status of teachers has hardly improved and may even have declined" (p. 35).

In the European Union, the pay level is much variable. In Japan: "Teachers are still, by law, among the highest paid of Japan's civil servants. When they start their service, they are paid as well as novice engineers" (OECD 2011b, p. 145). Teachers' pay also played a significant role in Korea, where "a key part of the strategy over decades has been to attract great people into teaching by paying them excellently" (Barber et al. 2012, p. 44). In Finland, teachers' pay is at the national average and is equivalent to the average of OECD countries. However: "More important than salaries are such factors as high social prestige, professional autonomy in schools, and the ethos of teaching as a service to society and the public good" (Sahlberg 2010, p. 2).

- **Career Prospects**

One of the conclusions of the 2013 International Summit on the Teaching Profession was the following:

> There is an emerging consensus that the teaching career is too flat, and that to attract and keep talented teachers – as well as to strengthen instructional leadership within a school – appraisal systems should be linked to opportunities for outstanding teachers to play broader leadership roles in schools beyond their own classrooms. (Asia Society 2013, p. 23)

The House of Commons Report (2012) recommended designing a formal and flexible career structure with different paths and awards. "We believe that the introduction of such a structure would bring significant advantages to the recruitment and retention of high-quality teachers, and bring teaching into line with other graduate professions in this regard" (p. 52). According to the European Commission *Document* (2012):

> The recognition of a wider range of tasks and responsibilities for schools and teaching staff also calls for the creation of new roles – such as mentor of beginning and trainee teaching staff, co-coordinator of in-service education, and school project co-coordinator. […]
> Creating new positions with specific tasks and roles in addition to classroom teaching can increase horizontal career differentiation; a career ladder that recognizes extra responsibilities, where access to each stage is more demanding, entails more responsibilities and a tighter selection, but also a higher status and remuneration. (p. 31)

The career structure may include a path of advancement through a hierarchy of excellence levels; a path of specialization in teaching areas; a path of acceding to direction posts in school; and paths open to other possibilities. In Singapore, for instance, a teacher may become Master Teacher, Curriculum Expert or Principal.

- **Evaluation**

Teachers' evaluation may be mandatory or voluntary, depending on the purpose. It may take place on specific occasions or periodically, "every 3–5 years at a minimum, more frequently if serious weaknesses require correction". It may be tied to periodic recertification, i.e. "a process by which teachers who are already working in the school system renew their teaching licence at regular intervals" (World Bank 2012, p. 96).

The aims, instruments and moments of a teacher evaluation or appraisal are varied:

> While teacher appraisals can have various purposes, nearly all are intended to improve teaching performance and/or strengthen accountability.
> Teacher appraisal for improvement, also referred to as developmental appraisal or formative appraisal, provides feedback that aims to help improve teaching practices, largely through professional development. It is usually conducted by the individual school and may not always be regulated nationally. By identifying individual teachers' strengths and weaknesses, teachers and school leaders can make more informed choices about the specific professional-development activities that best meet teachers' needs in the context of the school's priorities.
> Teacher appraisal for accountability, also referred to as summative appraisal, focuses on holding teachers accountable for their performance. (OECD 2013, p. 16)[26]

Appraisal for accountability or summary appraisal reflects a conception of the school disregarding its global mission as an institution for human flourishing, responsible citizenship and the common good. The curriculum is increasingly narrowed, and teachers are pressured by what is tested. The neoliberal reformers focus on instrumental knowledge and standardized testing. They "maintain that all children can attain academic proficiency without regard to poverty, disability, or other conditions, and that someone must be held accountable if they do not. That someone is invariably their teachers" (Ravitch 2012). Teachers are treated as a kind of *curriculum ventriloquists*, evaluated on the basis of students' scores in standardized tests. Their evaluation tends to pulverize the teaching profession into a paraphernalia of static indicators, becoming a kind of *Gray's Anatomy*, to satisfy an insatiable paperwork bureaucracy. The use of so-called value-added methods (VAMs) aims at measuring gains in test scores in the teacher's class over time.

> However, it is difficult to identify the specific contribution a given teacher makes to a student's performance. Learning is influenced by many factors: the student's own skills, expectations, motivation and behaviour; the support students receive from their families and the influence of their peer group; school organisation, resources and climate; and curriculum structure and content. The effect that teachers have on a student's performance is also cumulative: at any given moment, a student is influenced not only by his or her current teachers but also by former teachers. Raw standardised scores thus reflect much more than the impact of a single teacher on student performance (Isoré 2009). (OECD 2013, p. 35)

---

[26] Accountability is an ancient English term whose etymology is 'count', but has gained a broader meaning that entered the dictionaries and encyclopedias only in the 1980s, following Dario Castiglione (2006).

Following the ILO *Handbook* (2012):

> [T]eacher evaluation should have as its central goal the improvement of teaching and learning. Within this perspective, an emphasis should be placed on the reward of good practices, as much as on the improvement of weaker ones. Such appraisal should be largely diagnostic and formative, identifying weaknesses in skills and competencies, and should be holistic, based on all variables in the school setting which affect teaching and learning (ILO 2000a). [...]
>
> The process of evaluating teachers begins with a planning and preparation stage to determine baseline data or reference marks and to clarify and communicate criteria and procedures. It will not end before the assessment results or feedback are communicated, all clarification or appeals procedures are exhausted [...] and the necessary post-evaluation training to improve performance and correct weaknesses has been completed. The process usually utilizes a range of methods and tools of obtaining information about teacher performance including:
>
> – classroom observations;
> – interviews with the teacher, either one to one or with a panel;
> – self-evaluation questionnaire for the teacher;
> – the teacher's qualifications, for example if professional development activities have been undertaken, can also be used as an assessment tool and be part of the evaluation criteria questionnaire to students; and
> – the use of teacher portfolios based on a range of teacher activities, in print or video format. (pp. 90, 95)

Teachers' appraisal may also include peer and school-leader evaluation, students and parents surveys, external evaluation by authorities, and student-performance test scores. The World Bank *Framework* (2012) affirms: "Using multiple sources to assess teacher performance is crucial, since no method of evaluating teachers is failsafe. [...] Therefore, it is crucial to use as many sources of information on teacher performance as possible so that they complement each other and produce a more accurate evaluation of their work (Grossman et al. 2010)" (p. 29).

According to an EI survey:

> [F]or appraisal schemes to have value and to contribute to the quality of education, teachers need to be able to trust them and to consider them fair. [...] In addition, the evidence is that for appraisal to be trusted and considered fair a range of evidence should be taken into account. When teacher appraisal arrangements and policies are devised with the participation of teachers and their unions, comprehensive methods seem to be able to gain teachers' trust and provide more valuable information. (Figazzolo 2013, p. 48)

For example:

> As part of its efforts to professionalize teaching, Ontario ended several policies adopted in the 1990s, such as testing and evaluation requirements that teachers had seen as punitive, which had led to an exodus from the profession. The incoming Liberal government, which took office in 2003, instead created a Working Table on Teacher Development that included teacher representatives, and adopted policies aimed at providing support and building teachers' capacity to teach more effectively. (Darling-Hammond and Rothman 2011, p. 7)[27]

---

[27] An OECD (2011b) Report comments: "Given the 'teacher-bashing' engaged in by the previous government, this show of trust in the competence and professionalism of the teaching force was an

It should be noted that in Finland (and some other countries) there is no formal and external evaluation of teachers, which is a local responsibility.[28]

Here are the principal conclusions of the Amsterdam 2013 Summit concerning the evaluation of teacher quality:

> There was absolute agreement about the urgency of advancing in each country a shared vision of what the outcomes of education should be and that they should focus on cognitive, interpersonal, and intrapersonal outcomes. This shared vision should guide the continued collaborative work of government and teachers' union leaders in the ambitious task of improving schools. All policies and programmatic initiatives to support teaching and learning should be aligned with that shared vision. […]
>
> It was also unanimously understood that producing quality teaching is the responsibility of the profession of teachers, and that it is essential that teachers be engaged in defining the mechanisms to produce improvements in teaching. This would begin with the establishment or updating of standards that define teaching quality […].
>
> Doing justice to the multidimensional nature of teaching quality will require data from multiple sources of information and multiple stakeholders. […]
>
> Developing teacher-evaluation systems should not be like the single-minded pursuit of the Holy Grail or alchemist's stone; it is one of a series of policy tools that together can create a high-quality profession. To reprise the lessons from the first two Summits, the highest-performing systems are those that make teaching an attractive and respected career that invites the best candidates; provides high-quality initial teacher education, good mentoring, effective professional development and attractive career structures; and where teachers work collaboratively with school leaders in the design and implementation of reforms and innovations. In this context, teacher evaluation can be a critical lever. […]
>
> Teacher-appraisal systems are still a work in progress. Despite strongly held views, there is little research as yet on how well they work to improve teaching or learning. (Asia Society 2013, pp. 22...25)

• Public Image

An example of the importance of the teaching profession's public image is the SPARK programme launched in Norway in 2009.

> SPARK brings together the Ministry of Education, teachers unions, and organizations representing teacher education and school leaders at both national and regional levels. As a result of this collaboration, positive portrayals of the teaching profession in the media rose from 14 percent in 2008 to 59 percent in 2010, and in 2011, the number of applications to teacher education institutions increased by 38 percent and included a significant increase in the number of male applicants. (Asia Society 2011, p. 22)

(Footnote 27 continued)

essential ingredient in repairing the rupture that had developed between the profession and the government" (p. 76).

[28] In connexion with this, the Report of the 2013 International Summit on the Teaching Profession notes:

> Jaakko Meretniemi, a teacher from Finland, struck a different note. He said that teachers in Finland are well educated – all have master's degrees. He did not see the need for a formal teacher-evaluation system. Teachers get plenty of feedback from their students and colleagues. He worried that the Summit was going in the wrong direction, that increasing teacher inspections might kill teachers' passion for their work. (Asia Society 2013, p. 17).

The House of Commons Report (2012) recommended promoting the teaching profession's public image, as did the Teacher Training Agency campaign *No-one forgets a good teacher*, "with the explicit aim of increasing the number of applicants for each training position, and that marketing should communicate that teaching is rewarding in all senses of the word" (p. 50).

In any case, the teaching profession's public image is not a mere marketing challenge. In Finland, it became an admired and desirable profession because it is regarded "as a noble, prestigious profession—kin to medicine, law, or economics—and one driven by moral purpose rather than material interests" (Sahlberg 2010, p. 1). As the Report of the New York 2012 Summit also reads, "the high respect with which teachers are held and the considerable professional autonomy they enjoy accounts for the popularity of teaching as a profession" in Finland (Asia Society 2012, p. 13).

• **School Management**

Following the European Commission *Document* (2012):

> School leadership is second only to teaching among the school-related factors that determine what students learn and how successfully. It is an issue to which policymakers in several Member States need to pay closer attention, if educational institutions and systems are to achieve their maximum potential.
> The impact of educational leadership on student attainment is clear; some research shows that leadership accounts for 27 % of the variation in student achievement across schools. [...]
> The impact of school leaders tends to be stronger where there is a higher degree of school autonomy. However, systems vary significantly in the extent to which school principals can, for example, select the staff they are expected to lead, or adjust the school curriculum to local needs. (p. 43)

According to the World Bank *Framework* (2012):

> Having strong school leaders is fundamental. First, quality principals tend to attract and retain good quality teachers (Boyd et al. 2009; Ingersoll 2001a, 2001b). Second, capable principals can also spearhead much-needed change at the school level. Therefore, having strong leaders is important not only to ensure acceptable levels of performance but also to drive improvements. Finally, good principals can make a teacher's job easier. The more capable a principal, the more he or she can support teachers, create a sense of community, make teachers feel valued and ease their anxiety about external pressures (Mulford 2003). (p. 26)

The duties and influence of principals, directors and head teachers require their selection and preparation to see beyond mere administrative and managerial duties, as the school's autonomy (when it exists) depends mostly on them.

> Almost everywhere, professional teaching experience is the basic condition for appointment [to these positions]. The amount of experience required ranges from three to thirteen years and is generally between three and five years. In most countries, additional conditions are applied, which may include administrative experience, leadership and management competencies, the completion of special training courses. (p. 47)

For example, in Ontario, in 2008, a leadership strategy was initiated that included a principals' qualification program (PQP), mandatory for principals and

vice principals, accredited by the Ontario College of Teachers. It is provided by
faculties of education and by principals' associations, and consists of two parts,
each totalling 125 h, plus a practicum. In Singapore, after a demanding selection
process, potential school leaders are required to attend a six month leaders in
education program (LEP) conducted by the National Institute of Education.

• **Conclusion**

"While the educator-development systems of Finland, Ontario, and Singapore differ
in significant ways, what they have in common is that they are just that—*systems*
for teacher and leader development" (Darling-Hammond and Rothman 2011, p. 2).
The internal consistency of the approach to teaching profession is highlighted in the
World Bank *Framework* (2012) too, which "extracts principles and guidelines from
the research evidence to date on teacher policies, as well as the teacher policies of
high performing education systems".

> Based on a detailed review of the characteristics of successful education systems, the
> SABER-Teachers team identified four ways, or 'profiles', via which high performing
> systems combine the 8 Teacher Policy Goals to achieve good education results: 1. pro-
> fessional autonomy; 2. shared responsibility; 3. career development; and 4. performance
> management. […]
> Some high performing education systems place greater emphasis on providing extremely
> well qualified teachers with ample autonomy, while others decide to control more closely
> all aspects of teachers' work. […] Education systems like Finland that decide to grant
> ample autonomy to their teachers can do so without sacrificing the quality of education
> because they have well functioning mechanisms to ensure that there is an extremely well
> qualified teacher in every classroom. Education systems like Ontario that have less focus on
> attracting the best into teaching, focus instead on providing extensive support through
> teacher professional development and school leadership. Whatever profile high performing
> education systems choose, they ensure that the elements of the teacher policy sub-system
> are well aligned. (pp. 43, 44)

In short:

> Appropriately qualified, well-supported and remunerated, highly motivated teaching per-
> sonnel working in a stimulating teaching and learning environment are the most important
> element of any education system. The status of teachers and public esteem for the teaching
> profession are crucial to high-quality education delivery. (ILO 2012, Foreword)

Given its largely degraded status and the revolution of technologies of information and communication, another issue is emerging: Does the teaching profession have a future?

5.5 Future

The future of the teaching profession is obviously tied to that of the school.

Asking about the future of school, MacBeath (2012), after examining six
potential scenarios projected by an OECD study in 2001, concluded:

In each of these six hypothetical scenarios, the school plays a role from occupying centre stage at one extreme to a place in the supporting cast on the other. Whether or not knowledge and skills may be gained in sites other than school, the powerful social and moral role of schooling should not be omitted from the equation. [...]

Drawing on the Einstein maxim that problems cannot be solved by thinking within the framework in which they were created, the future of schools, schooling and education may go in essentially two diverse directions – one, to extend their compass (a form of re-schooling), the other to move towards a more modest role as a co-ordinating hub, the centrepiece in a network of small, people-friendly, local-based community sites (a form of deschooling). (pp. 80, 86)

At the conclusion of the New York 2012 Summit, "the powerful social and moral role of schooling" was highlighted:

The conversation was not just about basic skills and knowledge but about developing a broader range of skills and dispositions including the development of imagination, critical thinking, cross-cultural and global awareness, civic and political engagement, creativity, ingenuity, and inventiveness. The importance of education for environmental sustainability, prosperity, jobs, equality, human rights, and peace were all referenced as important goals. This moral vision undergirds the discussion of the future of the teaching profession. (Asia Society 2012, p. 22)

The school mission regarding the culture of moral and civic values, which are more and more crucial for Humankind's ability to keep control of its powers and destiny, is taken in due account by the French Dulot Report (2012). Here are some of its conclusions and recommendations:

- There is a "sometimes consumerist relation with education", a "commodification" of education (p. 15) by the "liberal models that privilege the functioning of educational quasi-markets" (p. 23).
- It is necessary to reaffirm the responsibility and "central role of the State" for the school as "a national public service" (p. 29).
- The school should give up its "encyclopedic posture" since, at present, nothing is more important than "learning to learn" (p. 25).
- The school "is a place of instruction, of intellectual education and of values transmission, so much as of preparation for social and professional life" (p. 23).
- It is necessary to overcome "the sterile opposition between instruction and education" that are the "two legs" of the education system, which should also "transmit a broad humanistic, scientific and artistic culture" (p. 25).
- The school should open itself to—and legitimize—new apprenticeships concerning daily life (life skills or "education for..."), such as digital education, media education, health education, sexual life education, citizenship education, etc.
- The school is not just a political space, but is "a pre-civic space" where the new generations should learn "to get informed on political matters, to make judgments from the viewpoint of the general interest, to be concerned about the common good, justice and equality, to argue and to debate, to assume collective responsibilities", in particular through "participation in representative school bodies and/or in the school associative life" (p. 26).

- "The school is not only a place of learning but also a place of life. It should then take care to have a welcoming quality" (p. 41). It should be architecturally, ergonomically and humanly welcoming for students, their families and teachers.
- Moreover, it should be also a community centre, "a public service at the service of the public" (p. 42).

As far as the teaching profession in particular is concerned:

- "The school *malaise* (uneasiness) is felt by teachers too", many of them "suffer in practicing the profession". They have a "feeling of the depreciation of their profession and lack of social status", especially when they are "reduced to mere subordinates" (pp. 17, 19).
- It is important to recognize the "crucial character of the reconstruction of a quality teaching education. An education that shall give to its professionalizing dimension all the importance it demands, besides the indispensable academic knowledge. Matter and manner. Teaching is a demanding job to be learned" (p. 31). Teaching education should be at the Master's level.

The "moral vision" is a hallmark of the Japanese education system.

> Again and again, the Japanese have asserted that the most important dimension of their system is the moral dimension: how people should behave and how they should relate to one another. The entire curriculum is suffused with the moral education agenda of the Japanese government. Though there are courses on moral education in primary schools, this agenda extends far beyond them. (OECD 2011b, p. 151)

As a consequence, one hardly conceives of societies without an institution where the new generations meet, with their diversity, to learn fundamental values and knowledge. The basic common school should be increasingly a school of the right to education as a right to learn, to learn to learn, to learn to be human and to live humanely, that is, in dignity and with solidarity, creativity, responsibility.

Moreover, schools should be prepared to serve not only students during the day but the whole community thereafter.

> [S]chools can become resource centres for community development (Field, Kuczera and Pont 2007). They can work closely with community health, recreation, youth, police and other local institutions to address external obstacles to learning. In some education systems, schools offer on-site professionals who provide complementary services directly to students and their parents. Evidence shows that such extensions of school services attract families that would otherwise be unwilling to be involved. The initiative Century Community Learning Center Program, in the United States, is one example. It aims to transform schools into community centres by providing extracurricular activities and supplementary instruction in reading for all. (OECD 2014, p. 94)

A school concerned with its global mission is yet to come. Jan Amos Comenský (Comenius in Latin) (1592–1670) already dreamed of it in *Didactica Magna* (The Great Didactic), Chapter XI[29]:

---

[29] http://core.roehampton.ac.uk/digital/froarc/comgre/.

1. … I call a school that fulfils its function perfectly, one which is a true forging-place of men; where the minds of those who learn are illuminated by the light of wisdom […]; in a word, where all men are taught all things thoroughly [*ubi omnes, omnia, omnino, doceantur*].
2. But has any school either existed on this plane of perfection or held this goal in view; not to ask if any has ever reached it? Lest I should seem to chase Platonic ideas and to dream of perfection such as exists nowhere and cannot be hoped for in this life, I will point out by another argument that such schools ought to be and have never existed.

Victor Hugo also dreamed of a school like that[30]:

Some day when men will be wise
And birds no longer through the cage are taught
When misshapen societies will feel,
In children better understood, their brows lift
That, from free flight having fathomed the rules,
The eagle's law of growth will be known
And high noon will shine for all
Knowledge being sublime, learning will be sweet.

What kind of teachers will future schools require?

Teachers should be a kind of professionals up to the challenges of the whole human resonance of education and the civilizational mission of the school.

The classical search for *good education* is the axis of the history of pedagogical thought, so much as the classical search for *good government* is the axis of the history of political thought. In this respect, Nathan Tarcov observed that "philosophers have been able to stand out in the realms of both educational theory and political theory ever since the two fields of thought first flowed from their common fountainhead, the *Republic* of Plato" (as cit. in Aldrich 1995). The primacy and interdependency of politics and education are illustrated by utopian literature: social utopias are always political–pedagogical, aiming both at a 'new society' and a 'new man'. Plato's (1997) *Republic* elaborates on a "city and the man who is like it" (541b).

Sigmund Freud (1856–1939) wrote in his preface to August Aichhorn's book *Verwahrloste Jugend* (Wayward Youth 1925): "At an early stage I had accepted the *bon mot* (witticism) which lays it down that there are three impossible professions —educating, healing and governing" (as cit. in Britzman 2009, p. 128). This idea is recalled in his paper "Analysis Terminable and Interminable" (*Die endliche und die unendliche Analyse*, 1937). Earlier, Kant (1803) had also said: "There are two human inventions which may be considered more difficult than any others, the art of government, and the art of education; and people still contend as to their very means" (para. 12). However, "the greatest and most difficult problem to which man can devote himself is the problem of education" (p. 11).

Plato (1997), considering in the *Laws* that education is "just about the most important activity of all" (803d), concluded that "the official that has the hardest job of all" is "the Director of Children" (813c). In the "Greeting to the Reader" of *The*

---

[30] Translation: http://unesdoc.unesco.org/images/0012/001202/120260e.pdf (p. 123).

Great Didactic, Comenius quoted "Philip Melanchthon who remarked that to educate the young well was a greater feat than to sack Troy", as well as Gregory Nazianzen who said: "To educate man is the art of arts, for he is the most complex and the most mysterious of all creatures" (para. 5). In his *Émile* (1762), Rousseau (1993a) regretted that "the most useful of all arts, the art of training men, is still neglected" (*la première de toutes les utilités, qui est l'art de former des hommes, est encore oubliée*) (Preface).

Rousseau (1993b) wrote in *Du Contrat Social* (The Social Contract, 1762), Chapter IV, Book III: "If we take the term in the strict sense, there never has been a real democracy, and there never will be. [...] Were there a people of gods, their government would be democratic. Such perfect government is not for men" (pp. 239, 240). A similar idea was expressed by Kant (1803) concerning education: "Were some being of higher nature than man to undertake our education, we should then be able to see what man might become" (p. 6). At the core of education's unique complexity and difficulty lies the Gordian Knot highlighted by Kant: "It is noticeable that man is only educated by man—that is, by men who have themselves been educated" (p. 6). Therefore, "insight depends on education, and education in its turn depends on insight" (p. 11).[31] How is it possible to solve the *aporia* (literally: "without passage") of Humankind having to educate itself? We hardly find in the history of the pedagogical thought a better approach than that of Kant who taught.

- "Man is the only being who needs education" (p. 1), because he "can only become man by education. He is merely what education makes of him" (p. 6).
- The educational vision should be inspired by the "principle" following which "children ought to be educated, not for the present, but for a possibly improved condition of man in the future; that is, in a manner which is adapted to the idea of humanity and the whole destiny of man" (p. 14).
- This implies an enlightened conception of a good education.

> If education is to develop human nature so that it may attain the object of its being, it must involve the exercise of judgment. Educated parents are examples which children use for their guidance. If, however, the children are to progress beyond their parents, education must become a study, otherwise we can hope for nothing from it, and one man whose education has been spoiled will only repeat his own mistakes in trying to educate others. The mechanism of education must be changed into a science, and one generation may have to pull down what another had built. (pp. 13, 14)

---

[31] Karl Marx (1818–1883) put it this way in "Theses on Feuerbach", first published as an appendix to *Ludwig Feuerbach and the End of Classical German Philosophy* (1886): "The materialist doctrine concerning the changing of circumstances and upbringing forgets that circumstances are changed by men and that it is essential to educate the educator himself". (www. marxists.org/archive/marx/works/download/Marx_Ludwig_Feurbach_and_the_End_of_German_ Classical_Philosop.pdf). This is a problem similar to the political one highlighted by Tom Campbell (2006): "The eternal problem of political philosophy is how we can guard the guardians" (p. 100).

- As a consequence, an education fit to bringing us "one step towards the perfecting of mankind" (p. 7) should be entrusted by each generation to "people of
  broader views, who take an interest in the universal good, and who are capable
  of entertaining the idea of a better condition of things in the future, that the
  gradual progress of human nature towards its goal is possible" (p. 17). Such
  people are likely the best human beings of each generation, as Plato (1997)
  suggested in the *Laws*:

  > Man is a 'tame' animal, as we put it, and of course if he enjoys a good education and
  > happens to have the right natural disposition, he's apt to be a most heavenly and gentle
  > creature; but his upbringing has only to be inadequate or misguided and he'll become the
  > wildest animal on the face of the earth. That's why the legislator should not treat the
  > education of children cursorily or as a secondary matter; he should regard the right choice
  > of the man who is going to be in charge of the children as something of crucial importance,
  > and appoint as their Minister the best all-round citizen in the state. (766a)

The American Report *Tomorrow's Teachers* affirmed: "Only the best and brightest
should be entitled to teach" (The Holmes Group 1986, p. 25). The prevailing
rhetoric on the teaching profession's quality does emphasize the need to attract *the
best*, but the best are not always meant to be the best persons as well. The House of
Commons Report (2012) affirms: "The impact of the best—and worst—teachers is
dramatic: there is a moral imperative to improve teaching yet further and to ensure
that there is only room in our system for the very best" (p. 5). Following the
conclusions of the aforementioned 2010 meeting of OECD Ministers of Education[32]: "We also need to focus our teacher selection on attracting the best to the
teaching profession". However: "Several countries pointed to the difficulty of
attracting those with the right mix of skills and personality into the teaching profession". To get teachers of such calibre is the challenge for the future. What kind of
professionals should they be?

- For millennia, schools and teachers have been the main sources of knowledge,
  especially when there were no books or they were very scarce. Teachers were
  professionals of knowledge.
- These days, the scientific-technological revolution and the multiplication of, and
  democratization of access to, the sources of knowledge are putting within reach
  of an increasing number of human beings a planetary library, affecting the
  traditional mission of school and the typical role of teachers. They are
  becoming, rather, *professionals of knowing how to learn*.
- Powers generated by the scientific-technological revolution raised new potential
  dangers demanding from human beings a conscience and wisdom that confer to
  the ethical, civic and international dimensions of school education an importance as great, at least, as that of its intellectual and professional role traditionally prevailing. Furthermore, as human beings become freer from the
  constraints of meeting their daily basic needs, they become more aspiring of
  higher levels of human life. Consequently, whatever the "miracles" of the

---

[32] www.oecd.org/dataoecd/53/16/46335575.pdf.

scientific-technological age may be, societies will need an educational institution whose professionals are primarily *professionals of learning to be*.[33]

- Professionals of learning to be should be *professionals of example*. Teachers' professional exemplarity is not to be reduced to a conservative moral connotation, but rather understood as an exceptional incarnation of a blend of qualities, values and knowledge. Personal qualities the teaching profession demands are emotional, moral and intellectual: qualities of kindness, empathy, relationality, serenity and openness—qualities of rigour and utopia. They arouse respect and admiration, exerting a positive lasting and resonant influence.

As a consequence, in spite of its current declining status in most countries of the world, and of the revolution of technologies of information and communication, the teaching profession has a future. Its future does not rely, however, on the technological illusion, that is, on the belief that *technological protheses* may bypass educators' as *persons*. The key principle of the pedagogical method will remain interpersonal communication. The human beings educators are—this is their most resounding influence in lives of children, adolescents and youth passing by them. That is why personal qualities and example are a classical theme in the history of pedagogical thought. Teachers' Professional Ethics often refer to their example as powerful "role models".[34] As Albert Einstein (1879–1955) is quoted as having said: "Example isn't another way to teach, it is the only way to teach".[35]

And what about parents?

Jean Baechler (1994) remarks that "the modernity emerging since the seventeenth century, first in Europe, thereafter worldwide, is a gigantic historical process of transcription of democracy into the different orders, and that such transcription is not yet finished". He noticed "a grave exception: children. Just as they are not free to not be born, so they are not free to choose their parents" (pp. 82, 83).

How can children become better than their parents?

In the *Republic*, Plato (1997) proposed the following:

---

[33] *Learning to be—The world of education today and tomorrow* is the title of an influential Report prepared by an International Commission appointed by UNESCO, published in 1972.

[34] For instance, the Teachers' Code of Ethics and Practice of the Council for the Teaching Profession in Malta, adopted in 2012, which elaborates on six "Key Principles", refers three times to 'role model' (defined as "any person who serves as an example and whose behaviour is emulated by others"), namely: "A teacher shall endeavour to be a role model and shall act within the community in a manner which enhances the prestige of the profession". Teachers should "behave in keeping with their unique position of trust and status as role models". They shoul:

Be mindful of their position as a role models to students; and
Both in their personal and professional life, be mindful of their behaviour and attitude, being that these may have an impact on the profession they represent.

(http://education.gov.mt/en/resources/documents/teachers%20resources/teachers%20code%20of%20ethics%20en.pdf).

[35] www.alberteinsteinsite.com/quotes/einsteinquotes.html.

It follows from our previous agreements, first, that the best men must have sex with the best women as frequently as possible, while the opposite is true of the most inferior men and women, and, second, that if our herd is to be of the highest possible quality, the former's offspring must be reared but not the latter's. [...]

They [the true philosophers] will send everyone in the city who is over ten years old into the country. Then they'll take possession of the children, who are now free from the ethos of their parents, and bring them up in their own customs and laws, which are the ones we've described. This is the quickest and easiest way for the city and constitution we've discussed to be established, become happy, and bring most benefit to the people among whom it's established. (459d, 541a)

In the First Book (Chapter XXIII) of *Gargantua and Pantagruel* (François Rabelais, 1494–1553),[37] one reads:

When Ponocrates [schoolmaster] knew Gargantua's vicious manner of living, he resolved to bring him up in another kind; but for a while he bore with him, considering that nature cannot endure a sudden change, without great violence. Therefore, to begin his work the better, he requested a learned physician of that time, called Master Theodorus, seriously to perpend, if it were possible, how to bring Gargantua into a better course. The said physician purged him canonically with Anticyrian hellebore, by which medicine he cleansed all the alteration and perverse habitude of his brain. By this means also Ponocrates made him forget all that he had learned under his ancient preceptors, as Timotheus did to his disciples, who had been instructed under other musicians.

Platonic totalitarian bio-political eugenics must never come into being, and there is no *Anticyrian hellebore* able to make children forget the wrongs of their education. The *secret* of overcoming the Gordian Knot of the self-perfecting of Humankind through the education of its children is, rather, a desirable and possible *ethical eugenics*, "by fostering their best part with our own" (*Republic*, 590d).

To summarize: The best education is one that is illuminated by the best idea of human perfection, guided by the best knowledge on human and individual nature, and entrusted to the best human beings. To attract the best to the education professions:

- The personality of education professionals being the core of their professional identity, they should be selected, educated and evaluated accordingly, and education recognized and esteemed as the most personally demanding and socially far-reaching profession.
- Teachers should be those principally responsible for attracting the best human beings to their profession. How? by means of outstanding professional self-governing bodies, i.e. composed of people holding a passionate and inspiring vision of the teaching profession.

---

[37] www.gutenberg.org/ebooks/1200.

References

Aldrich, R. (1995). John Locke (1632–1704). In UNESCO, *Penseurs de l'éducation—Volume 3* (pp. 65–82). Paris: UNESCO/BIE. www.ibe.unesco.org/fileadmin/user_upload/archive/publications/ThinkersPdf/lockee.PDF.

Aristotle. (1925). *The Nicomachean ethics* (Translated with an Introduction by David Ross, Revised by J. L. Ackrill and J. O. Urmson). Oxford: University Press (1998).

Asia Society. (2011). *The international summit on the teaching profession—improving teacher quality around the world.* http://asiasociety.org/files/lwtw-teachersummitreport0611.pdf.

Asia Society. (2012). *The 2012 international summit on the teaching profession—teaching and leadership for the twenty-first century.* http://asiasociety.org/files/2012teachingsummit.pdf.

Asia Society. (2013). *The 2013 international summit on the teaching profession—teacher quality.* http://asiasociety.org/files/teachingsummit2013.pdf.

Bæchler, J. (1994). *Précis de la démocratie.* Paris: Calman-Lévy/Éditions UNESCO.

Barber, M., Donnelly, K., & Rizvi, S. (2012). *Oceans of innovation—the Atlantic, the Pacific, global leadership and the future of education.* London: Institute of Public Policy Research. www.ippr.org/images/media/files/publication/2012/09/oceans-of-innovation_Aug2012_9543.pdf.

Britzman, D. P. (2009). *The very thought of education: psychoanalysis and the impossible professions.* New York: State University of New York.

Campbell, E. (2008). Teaching ethically as a moral condition of professionalism. In L. Nucci & D. Narvaez (Ed.), *International handbook of moral and character education.* New York and London: Routledge. Retrieved January 2013 from http://sitemaker.umich.edu/tei/files/campbell_teaching_ethically.pdf.

Campbell, T. (2006). *Rights—A critical introduction.* London: Routledge.

Castiglione, D. (2006). Accountability. In *Encyclopedia of governance.* California: SAGE Publications.

Darling-Hammond, L., & Rothman, R. (2011). Lessons learned from Finland, Ontario, and Singapore. In L. Darling-Hammond, & R. Rothman (Ed.), *Teacher and leader effectiveness in high-performing education systems* (pp. 1–11). Washington, DC: Alliance for Excellent Education and Stanford Center for Opportunity Policy in Education. www.all4ed.org/files/TeacherLeaderEffectivenessReport.pdf.

Department for Education. (2010). *The importance of teaching—the schools white paper 2010.* Presented to Parliament by the Secretary of State for Education by Command of Her Majesty, November 2010. www.education.gov.uk/publications/eOrderingDownload/CM-7980.pdf.

Dulot, A. et al. (2012). *Refondons l'École de la République—Rapport de la concertation.* www.refondonslecole.gouv.fr/wp-content/uploads/2012/10/refondons_l_ecole_de_la_republique_rapport_de_la_concertation1.pdf.

European Commission. (2012). *Supporting the teaching professions for better learning outcomes.* Commission Staff Working Document—Accompanying the Document: Communication from the Commission—Rethinking Education: Investing in Skills for Better Socio-Economic Outcomes (SWD (2012) 374 final). Retrieved July 2014 from http://eur-lex.europa.eu/LexUriServ/LexUriServ.do?uri=SWD:2012:0374:FIN:EN:PDF.

Figazzolo, L. (2013). *The use and abuse of teacher appraisal—an overview of cases in the developed world.* Brussels: Education International. http://download.ei-ie.org/Docs/WebDepot/TeacherAppraisal.pdf.

House of Commons. (2012). *Great teachers: attracting, training and retaining the best ninth report of session 2010–12, volume I: Report, together with formal minutes.* London: Education Committee. www.publications.parliament.uk/pa/cm201012/cmselect/cmeduc/1515/1515.pdf.

ILO. (2012). *Handbook of good human resource practices in the teaching profession.* Geneva: International Labour Organization—Sectoral Activities Department. www.ilo.org/wcmsp5/groups/public/—ed_dialogue/—sector/documents/publication/wcms_187793.pdf.

Immordino-Yang, M. (2009). Social neuroscience and its application to education. In S. Feifer, & G. Rattan (Eds.), *Emotional disorders: A neuropsychological, psychopharmacological, and educational perspective* (pp. 15–22). Middletown, MD: School Neuropsychology Press. Retrieved September 2012 from www.bcf.usc.edu/~immordin/papers/Immordino-Yang_2009_SocialNeuroscienceEdApplications.pdf.

Immordino-Yang, M. (2011). Implications of affective and social neuroscience for educational theory. *Educational Philosophy and Theory, 43*(1), 98–103. Retrieved September 2012 from www.bcf.usc.edu/~immordin/papers/Immordino-Yang_EPAT_2011.pdf.

Immordino-Yang, M., & Fischer, K. (2010). Neuroscience bases of learning. In V. G. Aukrust (Ed.), *International encyclopedia of education* (3rd ed., pp. 310–316). Oxford: Elsevier. Retrieved September 2012 from www-bcf.usc.edu/~immordin/papers/Immordino-Yang+Fischer_2009_NeuroscienceBasesofLearning.pdf.

Jetsonen, S. (2011). Setting the scene for learning. In *The best school in the world.* Helsinki: Museum of Finnish Architecture. http://issuu.com/suomen-rakennustaiteen-museo/docs/bestschoolintheworld_book#download.

Johansson, E. (2011). Introduction. In *The best school in the world.* Helsinki: Museum of Finnish Architecture. http://issuu.com/suomen-rakennustaiteen-museo/docs/bestschoolintheworld_book#download.

Kane, R., & Mallon, M. (2006). *Perceptions of teachers and teaching.* New Zealand: Ministry of Education. Retrieved January 2013 from www.teacherscouncil.govt.nz/research/percept-teachersteaching.pdf.

Kant, I. (1803). *On education* ('Über Pädagogik', Translated by Annette Churton, with an Introduction by C. A. Foley Rhys Davids, M.A.). Boston, U.S.A.: D. C. Heath and Co., Publishers, 1906. http://archive.org/details/kantoneducationu00kantuoft.

Leslie, C. (Ed.). (2013). *Towards a royal college of teaching—raising the status of the profession.* London: The Royal College of Surgeons of England. Retrieved July 2014 from http://filestore.aqa.org.uk/news/pdf/AQA-NEWS-TOWARDS-A-ROYAL-COLLEGE.PDF.

Lewin, K. (1951). *Field theory in social science: Selected theoretical papers by Kurt Lewin.* New York: Harper and Row.

MacBeath, J. (2012). *Future of teaching profession.* Education International Research Institute, University of Cambridge—Faculty of Education, Leadership for Learning—The Cambridge Network. http://download.ei-ie.org/Docs/WebDepot/EI%20Study%20on%20the%20Future%20of%20Teaching%20Profession.pdf.

McRuer, J. C. (1968–1971). *Report of the royal commission inquiry into civil rights—Report number one, volume.* Toronto: Queens' Printer.

National Commission on Excellence in Education. (1983). *A nation at risk: The imperative for educational reform (Washington).* http://datacenter.spps.org/uploads/SOTW_A_Nation_at_Risk_1983.pdf.

Nuikkinen, K. (2011). Learning spaces: How they meet evolving educational needs. In *The best school in the world.* Helsinki: Museum of Finnish Architecture. http://issuu.com/suomen-rakennustaiteen-museo/docs/bestschoolintheworld_book#download.

OECD. (2005). *Teachers matter—Attracting, developing and retaining effective teachers.* Paris: OECD Publishing.

OECD. (2011a). *Building a high-quality teaching profession—Lessons from around the world—Background report for the international summit on the teaching profession.* Paris: OECD Publishing. Retrieved January 2013 from www2.ed.gov/about/inits/ed/internationaled/background.pdf.

OECD. (2011b). *Strong performers and successful reformers in education—Lessons from PISA for the United States.* Paris: OECD Publishing. Retrieved June 2014 from www.oecd.org/pisa/46623978.pdf.

OECD. (2013). *Teachers for the 21st century—Using evaluation to improve teaching—Background report for the 2013 international summit on the teaching profession.* Paris: OECD Publishing. Retrieved April 2013 from www.oecd.org/site/eduistp13/TS2013%20Background%20Report.pdf.

OECD. (2014). *Equity, excellence and inclusiveness in education—Policy lessons from around the world*. Paris: OECD Publishing, by Andreas Schleicher. Retrieved June 2014 from http://teachfirstnz.org/images/uploads/Documents/OECD.pdf.

Pearson. (2012). *Lessons in country performance in education—2012 report*. London: The Learning Curve, Economist Intelligence Unit. http://thelearningcurve.pearson.com/the-report.

Plato. (1997). In: J. M. Cooper & D. S. Hutchinson (Eds.), *Complete works*. Indianapolis/Cambridge: Hackeht Publishing Company.

Ramsey, G. (2000). *Quality matters—Revitalising teaching: Critical times, critical choices—Report of the review of teacher education*. New South Wales. www.det.nsw.edu.au/teachrev/reports/reports.pdf.

Ravitch, D. (2012). *Schools we can envy. The New York Review of Book. 8 March*. Retrieved January 2013 from www.nybooks.com/articles/archives/2012/mar/08/schools-we-can-envy/?pagination=false.

Reboul, O. (1971). *La philosophie de l'éducation*. Paris: PUF (1981, 3è éd.).

Rousseau, J.-J. (1993a). *Émile* (Translated by Barbara Foxley, Introduction by P. D. Jimack). Vermont: Everyman (2004).

Rousseau, J.-J. (1993b). *The social contract and discourses* (Translated and introduced by G. D. H. Cole, updated by P. D. Jimack). Vermont: Everyman.

Royal Commission on Learning. (1995). *For the love of learning*. www.edu.gov.on.ca/eng/general/abcs/rcom/full/royalcommission.pdf.

Sahlberg, P. (2010). *The secret to Finland's success: Educating teachers*. Stanford University, School of Education, Stanford Center for Opportunity Policy in Education—Research brief. http://edpolicy.stanford.edu/sites/default/files/publications/secret-finland%E2%80%99s-success-educating-teachers.pdf.

Shulman, L. (2005). The signature pedagogies (Delivered at the math science partnerships (MSP) workshop: 'Teacher education for effective teaching and learning', hosted by the National Research Council's Center for Education, February 6–8, 2005, Irvine, California). Retrieved January 2013 from http://hub.mspnet.org/media/data/Shulman_Signature_Pedagogies.pdf?media_000000005488.pdf.

The Holmes Group. (1986). *Tomorrow's teachers*. New York. Retrieved January 2013 from www.canterbury.ac.uk/education/tf-mentors/ProfessionalDev/Documents/TomorrowsTeachers.pdf.

UNESCO. (1998). *World education report—1998—Teachers and teaching in a changing world*. www.unesco.org/education/information/wer/PDFeng/wholewer98.PDF.

Whitty, G. (2006). "Teacher professionalism in a new era", text of the first General Teaching Council for Northern Ireland Annual Lecture delivered at Queen's University, Belfast, March 14, 2006. Retrieved January 2013 from www.gtcni.org.uk/publications/uploads/document/Annual%20Lecture%20Paper.pdf.

World Bank. (2012). *What matters most in teacher policies?—A framework for building a more effective teaching profession*. Human Development Network, SABER: Systems Approach for Better Education Results. http://siteresources.worldbank.org/EDUCATION/Resources/278200-1290520949227/SABER-Teachers-Framework-Updated_June14.2012.pdf.

Part III
Self-regulation: A Bridge Between the Present and the Future of the Teaching Profession?

Chapter 6
Regulation of Professions

Abstract Professional self-regulation is a hallmark of the most socially relevant, responsible and recognized professions. It is the gold standard of professional status in most Anglo-Saxon countries, but in the rest of the world it has not been favoured by the centralized Nation States. Economic regulation means State intervention in the domain of economic–professional activities, in the public interest, that is, to protect consumers, clients and society in general from potential harm. Professional regulation basically consists in controlling the access to the practice of a profession by means of registration and certification or licensure, aiming at assuring that professionals provide services in a competent, ethical and safe manner, with the highest quality and at an affordable price. Professional self-regulation means, literally, the regulation of a profession by itself. It may be purely private, private but with some kind of official recognition, or public. It is public when operated by a professional body vested with statutory powers delegated by the Legislature. The basic self-regulatory powers and functions are registration and certification or licensure of the profession's members. The highest and most arduous mission of a self-regulatory body is adopting, cultivating and supervising respect for Professional Standards. Its supreme empowerment is the disciplinary one, which amounts to a judicial power. Professional self-regulation is sometimes objected to chiefly for the following reasons: it lacks democratic legitimacy; it is incompatible with freedom of association; it is inherently exposed to a potential conflict of interests; it is an obstacle to competition. Such objections either have no valid foundation or may be solved. Professional self-regulation brings benefits for all stakeholders. They may be summarized in four "P"s: public, professional, personal and political. Could the teaching profession be self-governing? What can teachers win with it?

Keywords Economic regulation · Professional self-regulation · Self-regulatory powers · Objections · Benefits

© The Author(s) 2015   103
A. Reis Monteiro, *The Teaching Profession*, SpringerBriefs in Education,
DOI 10.1007/978-3-319-12130-7_6

In 2011, the 6th Education International (EI) World Congress meeting in Cape Town, South Africa, adopted a "Resolution on the Future of the Teaching Profession".[1] Thereafter, EI asked John MacBeath to conduct a study that was published with the title *Future of the Teaching Profession*. The author asks: "What will be the nature of the professional identity and priorities for the next generation of teachers? What does it mean for change to be driven by the profession, by professional bodies and by essential professional values?" (MacBeath 2012, p. 93). After referring to "tensions between the conservative present and the radical future", he concludes that there is "a lot at stake", but there are "seeds of the future in the present" (pp. 98, 100).

Below I submit that self-regulation may be a royal route to higher professionality. In order to provide an elementary understanding of what is at stake, a brief introduction to economic–professional regulation is useful.

6.1 Economic–Professional Regulation

"Regulation" is a term with various uses. The management of life, its regulation or *homeostasis*, is "the primary function of human brains" (Damásio 2010, p. 63). At the sociopolitical level, regulation means action aiming at a state of desirable balance, with a normative texture, always implying some kind of coercion, to harmonize the plurality of interests and to make possible living together, communication, cooperation and the promotion of general well-being. The regulation of individual and group behaviours and activities, by means of rules and institutions, has always been a condition *sine qua non* of peaceful human communities. As Bæchler (1994) puts it: "'How to live together without killing one another?' Politics is the solution to that problem properly and exclusively human" (p. 25). In the economic field, regulation means State intervention in the domain of economic–professional activities, in the public interest, that is, to protect consumers/clients and society in general from potential harm. The greater the risks inherent to such activities are, the greater the necessity for regulation.

• Rationale

According to economic theory, the market should provide the best combination of quantity, quality and price of goods and services. If not, a "market failure" exists. As reads a report of the Canadian Competition Bureau (2007):

> In well-functioning markets, unfettered competition is the best means of ensuring that resources are allocated efficiently, that consumers have access to the broadest range of services at the most competitive prices and that producers have the maximum incentive to reduce their costs as much as possible and meet consumer demand. [...].

---

[1] http://pages.ei-ie.org/library/en/libraries/detail/159.

> Markets for professional services are potentially vulnerable to two main sources of market failure: asymmetric information and externalities. In the presence of such market imperfections, free markets may not generate efficient outcomes, which may be a rationale for regulation, based on protecting the public interest. (p. 17)

Asymmetric information arises when consumers/clients are not able to choose the right good/service with the right quality and at the right price, or to assess their quality. For example, a service provider may reduce the price by cutting quality. A distinction should be made between search, experience and credence goods/services that refers to their respective characteristics and the accuracy with which consumers can observe and evaluate them: *search goods* are those whose quality consumers are best able to evaluate before buying them; *experience goods* are those whose quality consumers only can evaluate upon consumption; *credence goods* are those whose quality consumers are not fully able to assess, even after consumption.

> This divide between buyers and sellers is perhaps the most important source of market failure in professional services markets and is the rationale regulators cite most for imposing restrictions in these markets.
> [...]
> Eyeglasses frames are an example of search goods, since consumers are able to determine whether the fit and style suit their preferences prior to purchase. The lenses that are made for the frames are likely experience goods: consumers can only determine whether their vision has become clearer by looking through the lenses for some time. Complete eye health exams are credence goods, since consumers would not know with certainty after all the tests whether the resulting diagnosis for poor vision was correct. (p. 18)

Externalities mean the effects of low-quality goods/services—either negative or positive—on third parties arising from decisions made by professionals or their clients. Examples: If a physician fails to diagnose a contagious disease, his incompetency may contribute to an epidemic; if a lawyer's pleading of a case before a court is incompetent or negligent, this may have negative effects, not just for his or her client, but also for the society as a whole; if incompetent teachers are hired to teach in public schools, this results in the detriment of students (and their parents that are taxpayers).

There are other sources of market failure, such as the dual role of performing the tasks both of diagnosing and solving. For example, an auto mechanic may provide fraudulent repairs or unnecessarily replace parts or charge for parts not actually replaced.

There are market deterrents and a non-market response for market failures. Market deterrents of market failures are, for example, the issue of guarantees, fear of bad reputation and threat of litigation. However, guarantees may have the effect of making the consumer less preventive, because of relying on them, incurring "moral hazard", i.e. taking risks whose possible costs will be charged to others. Reputation is associated with quality, but it tends to be reflected in higher prices. Litigation implies that the consumer is able to evaluate to some extent the quality of the good/service received and can afford the cost required. "In light of asymmetric information, potential externalities and the possibility of some services being akin to public goods, markets for professional services most likely require some form of regulation" (p. 20), i.e. non-market responses.

• Theories

There are two main theories explaining the demand for professional regulation: the public interest theory and the capture theory.

- Following the public interest theory, consumers have a great interest in being protected by State against bad professionals.
- Following the capture theory, professional regulation is, rather, driven by the pursuit of private interests, namely the privileges and higher incomes it carries.

The State has the right and the obligation to regulate professions whose services are vital for individuals and the whole society, as well as any others demanding guarantees for the public protection. For instance, the Constitution of the Portuguese Republic (1976, last revised in 2005) provides (Article 47—Freedom to choose a profession and of access to the public service):

> 1. Everyone has the right to choose a profession or type of work freely, subject to the legal restrictions that are imposed in the collective interest or the restrictions that are inherent in a person's own capabilities.

In European Union Member States, there are more than 800 regulated professions, that is, requiring certain formal qualifications.

Professional regulation consists basically in controlling the access to the practice of a profession by means of registration and certification or licensure, aiming at assuring that professionals provide services in a competent, ethical and safe manner, with the highest quality and at an affordable price.

The spectrum of the types of regulation ranges from being voluntary through to enforcement of a public regime. As public professional regulation consumes resources, as well as restricts market competition and individual choice, the decision to regulate a profession should imply:

- Assessing whether, because of the nature of the services it provides, the gross incompetency or professional misconduct of its professionals may put in danger life, health, safety, property, welfare or other goods and interests of their clients and of the public in general.
- Choosing the most appropriate form of regulation, which should be the most convenient for all interests at stake, namely the most favourable to enhancing the quality and diminishing the costs and prices of the professional services, and the most efficient and cost effective, balancing public protection with the public interest in a competitive services market place.

• Levels

The intensity of the regulation of a profession depends upon the nature of the services it provides and the damages it is able to cause if they are not properly provided. Professions whose services are the most vital for everyone and the society as a whole, with greater asymmetry between the professionals and the clients, should be more intensively regulated.

Regulation levels are principally the following, which are of growing demand and decreasing scope: registration, certification and licensure.

○ *Registration*

Registration is the least restrictive form of professional regulation. It consists simply in recording the names and addresses of people meeting the qualifications to exercise the profession, so informing the public about who is qualified to provide the respective services. In this case, the only deterrent from low-quality services is the threat of registration revocation. "The main deficiency of registration is that any professional could get away with at least one violation before being barred. Thus, this policy option may be undesirable when a single violation imposes significant harm, and the reduction in costs associated with moving to registration from licensing is small" (Cox and Foster 1990, p. 50).

○ *Certification*

Certification refers to the issuance of a certificate by a public or private regulatory body attesting to a person's attainment of specific education and training, becoming eligible to practise a profession. It is a form of professional regulation that affords *protection of title*. A professional title is protected when it may be used only by individuals to whom it is granted, without precluding practice by non-certified professionals.

Certification is advantageous for consumers in that it states that somebody has a proven expertise in a given field of services, but allows them to choose either a lower priced, non-certified professional, or a higher priced, certified one. However, a bad decision may result in significant costs and cause externalities. "States might require individuals to use certified professionals in situations where externalities are likely to be present and allow individuals to choose between certified and non-certified professionals when externalities are not present. [...] In addition, since the private sector may be more efficient than public regulatory boards, private certification systems may be an attractive alternative to licensing" (pp. 46, 49).

○ *Licensure*

Licensure refers to the issuance of a licence by a publicly mandated governing body, attesting to a person's attainment of the competency required to perform certain professional acts. It is the most restrictive form of professional regulation, as it amounts to a *reservation of practice*, granting thus a monopoly: licensed professions are those whose practice is forbidden to those who do not possess a professional title ensuring the practitioner meets the mandatory Professional Standards. Because of that, it cannot be a power entrusted to a private body.

According to some research, licensing may cause a decrease in supply, increases in prices and higher incomes for the members of the profession, while not necessarily increasing the quality of professional services, which depends on many other factors not controlled by licensing. For example, licensing does not guarantee the continued competence of the members of the profession, except if regular recertification is compulsory. And even if the quality of the licensed services increases, if the prices increase as well, consumers may switch to lower cost alternatives or choose to forgo services and become "do-it-yourselfers", incurring possible risks.[2] Therefore, if professional services' quality level is too high, it may revert to prejudice for consumers. "In general, we find that licensing is most likely to be beneficial when consumers cannot evaluate the quality of a professional's services. For example, persons needing emergency health care may benefit from licensing requirements" (pp. v, vi).

Accreditation is another term that is sometimes used as synonymous with registration, certification or licensure, but it is most frequently applied to the act of recognizing that a professional education programme complies with established standards.

The terminology of the levels of professional regulation is somewhat free-floating and sometimes overlapping and interchangeable, as one reads, for instance, in the Glossary of General Terminology used in Professional and Occupational Regulation of the Council on Licensure, Enforcement and Regulation (CLEAR), which is the principal international organization in the professional regulation field (located in Kentucky, USA, with an office in Bristol, UK).[3] An example is the Accord Policy on Registration/Licensing/Certification of the Practice of Architecture of the International Union of Architects (UIA)[4] that says: "For the sake of brevity, the term 'registration' is used throughout the guideline to denote 'registration/licensing/certification'". It begins with this definition:

> Registration/licensing/certification is the official legal recognition of an individual's qualification allowing her or him to practice as an independent architect, associated with regulations preventing unqualified persons from performing certain functions. Given the public interest in a high-quality, sustainable built environment and the dangers and consequences associated with the construction industry, it is important that architectural services are provided by properly qualified professionals in order to provide adequate protection for the public.

An alternative may be a combination of monitoring the quality of service with registration, certification or licensure, applied in an effective manner.[5] Another alternative to help consumers distinguish professionals' quality is requiring

---

[2] For example, one study found that stricter mandatory entry requirements for electricians "are significantly associated with a rise in the rate of death from accidental electrocution" (Cox and Foster 1990, p. 29).

[3] www.clearhq.org/resources/Glossary_General.pdf.

[4] www.mimarlarodasi.org.tr/UIKDocs/4.pdf.

[5] For example: "Individuals who perform television repairs in California are required to register with the State. Allegations of fraudulent repairs are investigated by a staff of trained professionals hired by the State" (Cox and Foster 1990, p. 48).

disclosure of relevant information, if the service performed is not too complex to be assessed by consumers (for example, the disclosure of an educator's criminal record). Consumers associations and other groups are also helpful in providing information on the quality of professionals' services. In short:

> In assessing whether regulation will benefit consumers and in determining the best regulatory framework – if regulation is needed – the characteristics of a particular market must be examined. Policy makers should consider the extent to which a potential market failure is likely to harm consumers. In particular, it is important to analyze: (1) the effectiveness of market and nonmarket responses to the problems created by market failure, and (2) the expected costs which will be incurred in the absence of regulation, and (3) the costs of any regulations, such as licensing, designed to cure the alleged market failure. (Cox and Foster 1990, p. 60)

• **Forms**

Once decided that a profession should be regulated, there are three basic methods of regulation:

- Direct: operated by Public Administration Departments.
- Indirect: allocated to a more or less autonomous statutory Agency/Authority.
- Delegated: entrusted to a self-governing body operating under public statute.

The diversity and complexity of Public Administration duties, on the one hand, and the interest and greater capacity of a profession to regulate itself, on the other, recommend self-regulation as a principle of political–administrative rationality.

6.2   Professional Self-regulation

Self-regulation is the gold standard of professional status in most Anglo-Saxon countries.

> Professions in Great Britain and other countries developed gradually from an unrestricted right to practise to professional self-regulation in the public interest. In the early 19th century virtually no controls existed to restrain those who called themselves a solicitor, a physician, or an accountant. [...]
> The professions have played a big role in the development of meritocracy because of their emphasis on knowledge-based skills rather than social class. (Spada 2009, pp. 11, 34)

Canada adopted the English tradition of professional self-regulation, which has spread into the Commonwealth,[6] and remains "the last bastion of unfettered self-regulation" (Rhode and Woolley, as cit. in Gorman 2014, p. 496). As the Law Reform Commission of Saskatchewan (2007) remarks: "At one time, only a few long-established traditional professions were self-governing. It is only in the last

---

[6] It is now an intergovernmental organization, formed by 53 member States, and most of them were former territories of the British Empire.

50 years that the self-governance model has been extended to a wide range of occupations and professions" (p. 3). Currently, there are a great number of professional self-regulatory bodies in the Canadian provinces. In most countries, self-regulation has been not favoured by the centralized Nation States.

• Rationale

Professional self-regulation means, literally, the regulation of a profession by itself. It may be purely private, private but with some kind of official recognition, or public. It is public when operated by a professional body vested with statutory public powers delegated by the Legislature.

Public self-regulation is the most appropriate form of regulation of a profession when it stands out with these main features:

- The profession is highly specialized and implies a margin of indetermination and unforeseeability requiring a high level of professional judgment, decision and responsibility.
- Given its expertise and the indetermination and unforeseeability of its practice, its professionals are in the best position to adopt Professional Standards and to identify and sanction unacceptable practice and conduct.
- The professional group is large enough to assume the organization and financing of its regulation, by means of a self-governing body separate from other professional associations.

In Saskatchewan (Canada), for example, a request for self-regulating status is measured against two sets of criteria: a primary set of 12 criteria that must be met and a secondary set of 10 criteria that are not decisive. The first mandatory requirement reads:

> 1. Whether the group requesting self-regulation will serve to protect the public against incompetence and misconduct that could affect the life, health, welfare, safety or property of the public and whether it is in the public interest that the group be given self-regulation (as cit. in Schultze 2007, p. 42).

In this respect, the McRuer Report (1968–1971) points out:

> The granting of self-government is a delegation of legislative and judicial functions and can only be justified as a safeguard to the public interest. The power is not conferred to give or reinforce a professional or occupational status. The relevant question is not, "do the practitioners of this occupation desire the power of self-government?", but "is selfgovernment necessary for the protection of the public?" No right of self-government should be claimed merely because the term "profession" has been attached to the occupation.
> [...]
> The traditional justification for giving powers of selfregulation to any body is that the members of the body are best qualified to ensure that proper standards of competence and ethics are set and maintained. There is a clear public interest in the creation and observance of such standards. (pp. 1162, 1166)

Professional self-regulation statute means, therefore, a contract between State and a profession: the profession is entrusted with powers peculiar to the sovereign authority of the State, in return for its commitment to prioritizing the clients' and general interests over its members' interests.[7]

The rationale of self-regulation is then the idea that the protection and advancement of the individual and public interests, including the affordability of services and the cost-effectiveness of regulation, are best served by the profession itself, if it complies with high Professional Standards.

• Powers and Functions

The mandate of a professional self-governing body may either be the minimal compatible with the very idea of self-regulation or very large. It may be entrusted with the following powers and functions:

- Registration
- Certification/Licensure
- Regulation that implies the following:

  - Adopting Professional Standards of fitness, competence, education practice and conduct, which may include the accreditation of initial and continuing professional education programmes.
  - Maintaining Professional Standards by means of, in particular:

    Mandatory continuing professional development.
    Disciplinary mechanisms—well known, client-friendly, fair and efficient —allowing for receiving and adjudicating complaints against members of the profession.

  - Other powers and functions such as launching or commanding research, offering programmes for continuing professional development, advising Government or other stakeholders on matters related to the profession, etc.

Therefore, the self-regulatory mandate includes three areas: administrative (related to the domestic management), legislative (related to public policies) and judicial (related to disciplinary powers). Its basic powers and functions are registration and certification or licensure of the profession's members. Its highest and most arduous mission is adopting, cultivating and supervising respect for Professional Standards. Its supreme empowerment is the disciplinary one, that is a judicial power.

Taking disciplinary action against professionals found guilty of serious incompetence or professional misconduct is crucial both for the profession and professionals. The proper enforcement and effectiveness of the disciplinary regime is a sound test and the touchstone of professional self-regulation's legitimacy and credibility. However, the disciplinary power must be surrounded by strong procedural safeguards necessary to respect for the rules of the so-called natural justice. As the British Columbia Court of Appeal stated, "the very nature of the proceedings

---

[7] In the UK, for example, the self-regulatory statute is traditionally granted through the award of a Royal Charter.

can have a devastating effect on a member's reputation, the single most valuable asset which any professional can possess (*Cameron v. Law Society* (*British Columbia*) 1991)" (as cit. in Schultze 2007, p. 50). The McRuer Report (1968–1971) recommended:

> The most obvious feature of the power of a self-governing body to discipline its members is that it is clearly a judicial power within the meaning we have given to that term, i.e. it consists of the independent and impartial application of predetermined rules and standards; no element of policy should be present in the exercise of this power. It is a power whose exercise may have the most far-reaching effects upon the individual who is disciplined. The sanction imposed upon one who has been found guilty of professional misconduct may be anything from a reprimand to expulsion from the profession.
> Where conviction may result in what has aptly and justifiably been termed "economic death", it is vital that procedural safeguards to ensure fairness be clearly established and rigorously observed. (p. 1181)

According to the Law Reform Commission of Saskatchewan (2007):

> The importance of procedural rules as a means of protecting the interests of the profession, the public, and the accused can hardly be overemphasized. Canadian courts have long required all disciplinary proceedings to follow what have been called the principles of natural justice. This was restated in very strong terms by the Supreme Court in a Saskatchewan case in 1990. [...]
> The standard model is a two-stage system:
>
> 1. When a complaint against a member is received, it is investigated by a committee of the association referred to in most of the governing statutes as the Investigation Committee, Professional Conduct Committee, or Ethics Committee. It will be referred to as the "Investigation Committee" in this handbook.
> 2. If the Investigation Committee concludes that misconduct or incompetence has occurred, the complaint is forwarded to a separate committee, the Discipline Committee. It is the Discipline Committee which presides over the formal discipline hearing. The Investigation Committee prosecutes the complaint and the accused member has an opportunity to be heard in defence. (pp. 4, 5)

• Objections

Professional self-regulation is sometimes objected to chiefly for the following reasons:

- it lacks democratic legitimacy;
- it is incompatible with freedom of association;
- it is inherently exposed to a potential conflict of interests; and
- it is an obstacle to competition.

Such objections either have no valid foundation or may be solved. It is not possible to address them at length here. It may be enough to remark that, if professional self-regulation is not losing any of its vitality, in general, it is because societies still see more benefits than disadvantages in the public contract underlying it. In fact, professional self-regulation brings benefits for all stakeholders, which may be summarized in four "P"s: public, professional, personal and political.

• **Benefits**

○ *Public Benefits*

When the State delegates regulatory powers in a profession, it is recognizing that the profession is in a better position to regulate itself and takes advantage of the profession being interested in it. In fact, the public interest and the interests of the members of a self-governing profession are not necessarily opposed. For example, professional competency is in the interest of the profession's prestige and of the public good. Moreover, society may trust the permanent conscience and competence of professionals more than regulatory agents of the Government of the day.

Consequently, if the exercise of a monopoly is inherent to professional self-regulation, it is also in the public interest, insofar as an atmosphere of confidence and of respect contributes to professional well-being and favours professionalism. As James Casey pointed out, "a vibrant, self-governing profession which has the public's interests at its heart is itself in the best interests of the public" (as cit. in Schultze 2007, p. 43). It is in that sense that "What's good for the Profession is good for the Public", that is, "the members of a content professional workforce are likely to feel more positive about their work and perform more effectively. There can also be a high degree of alignment between a profession and the public on high-quality standards in the sector in which a profession serves the public" (Kendel 2013, p. 12).

○ *Professional Benefits*

If professions, in general, aspire to a self-regulatory status, it is because they expect to obtain advantages from it. Indeed, professional self-regulation entrusts the profession with a power that brings prestige:

- the power to control the entrance into the profession and to supervise the professionalism of its members;
- the prestige resulting from the public trust, implied in that power, that is the greatest value of a profession.

In reality, if a profession pledges to respect high Professional Standards and the public knows that it can take action against professionals for incompetence and misconduct—the latter including conduct not becoming to a professional, not only conduct while on duty but also out of duty—this increases trust and confidence in the profession. Without inspiring trust and confidence, professionals cannot survive and a profession cannot flourish. They rely:

> ... on confidence of two kinds – the personal confidence of the patient or client in the technical competence of the practitioner, and the confidence of the public at large in the integrity and ethical conduct of the profession as a whole; the calling is one in which more than mere technical competence is required for the service of patients or clients and for the protection of the public, i.e. standards of ethical conduct must prevail; confidence is reposed in the practitioner, requiring that he does not exploit the intimate details of his patient's or

client's life and affairs which are divulged to him. No doubt many other characteristics of professions could be added. (McRuer 1968–1971, p. 1161)

○ *Personal Benefits*

As all things that give prestige to a profession return to benefit its professionals, they have a vested interest in self-regulation as a hallmark of professional status for the power it confers and the privilege it represents. In return, the proper functioning of a self-governing body depends upon the participation in its affairs of the professionals concerned. Furthermore, the manner in which they practice the profession reverberates in its dignity, prestige and social esteem. This was stressed by Denis Kendel (2013) in these terms: "The SMA [Saskatchewan Medical Association] and every doctor in the province would walk a mile over red-hot coals with bare feet before they would see the CPSS [College of Physicians and Surgeons of Saskatchewan] replaced by direct government regulation" (p. 57).

○ *Political Benefits*

Professional self-regulation is also beneficial for any Government because:

- Self-regulation is a kind of professional regulation with fewer political costs insofar as Governments are more insulated from, and less implicated in, professional issues that are within the statutory responsibilities of a self-governing body.
- Self-regulation is a kind of professional regulation prone to less conflict because the regulated are more confident and feel more responsible for the Professional Standards they themselves adopt and which are not imposed on them from outside the profession (thus better accepting the professional discipline).
- Self-regulation is a kind of professional regulation more flexible and efficient, as it is closer to the principal stakeholders than a more distant and bureaucratized entity, making it more agile to act and react, as well as more resilient and able to adapt to changes.
- Self-regulation is a kind of professional regulation less expensive for the public treasure because, being organized and financed by the profession itself, it avoids the costs of the information needed for its regulation and otherwise indispensable to its management; in fact, there is an informational asymmetry between governmental regulators and the regulated professionals that implies the former having to purchase professional expertise on a continuing basis.

It should be additionally noted that the final beneficiaries of professional self-regulation are, principally, the direct "clients" of the services of the profession.

The lobbying for professional self-regulation invokes the public interest, as already noted. The Code of Ethics of the Alabama State Bar Association goes so far as stating: "No sacrifice or peril, even to loss of life itself, can absolve from the fearless discharge" of the duty to act in the best interest of the client (para. 10).[8]

---

[8] www.sunethics.com/1887_code.htm.

Nonetheless, there is undoubtedly a risk of regulatory capture. The public interest may not coincide with professional self-interest, and regulators may place the interests of those they regulate ahead and above the interests of their clients and of the public in general. This is the case, for example, when inappropriate entry requirements into the professions are imposed and anti-competitive rules of conduct are enacted (as may be unreasonable restrictions on advertising). The exercise of the disciplinary power by the professionals may also be distorted by corporate solidarity.

As a consequence, since the 1980s, in some countries, the traditional model of self-regulation shifted. Two facts, in particular, called the paradigm of professional self-regulation into question, prompting significant changes in the regulatory landscape: the neoliberal wave and some professional scandals. The neoliberal wave pushed for a generalized economic deregulation, including the services market. It is claimed that excessive regulation hinders competition to the prejudice of clients and is an obstacle to economic growth. Professional scandals, involving doctors and lawyers[9] in particular, severely undermined public trust and confidence in professional self-regulation and pressured some Governments to intervene. The interventions took various forms and instruments. Parts of the self-regulatory powers (the disciplinary power, for instance) were removed, or professional self-governing bodies were brought under oversight by external regulation. Similar professions were grouped together under one piece of legislation. Examples are the *Legal Services Act* in England and Wales that groups seven categories of legal practitioners together, and the *Alberta Health Professions Act (Alberta, RSA2000, c. H-7)* that groups under one statute 28 categories of health practitioners, including physicians, administered by a Health Professions Advisory Board. The new configurations of professional regulation have been termed "meta-regulation" or "regulated self-regulation". Regulating the regulators means coregulation, that is, a shared task between governmental Authorities/Agencies and professions.

To prevent, as far as possible, the possibility of the power of professional self-regulation being misused, safeguards can be adopted, such as the following:

- Lay members should be appointed to the self-governing bodies in order for their monopolistic attributes not making the profession a "closed shop".[10]

---

[9] See, for instance, Dixon-Woods et al. (2011).

[10] In this respect, the Kendel Report (2013) observes:

> Over the past three decades there have been two major changes in the public's expectation of professional regulatory agencies. These relate to public engagement in regulatory processes and public transparency of those processes.
> Societal expectations of public engagement in professional regulation is most often achieved by having significant public participation on the governing boards, complaint investigation committees and discipline hearing committees of regulatory organizations. It is recommended that at least one third of the governing board be comprised of public members and that they have precisely the same powers and responsibilities as the professional members of the board. On complaint investigation committees, many professional regulatory organizations have an equal number of public and professional members. All

- The entrance into the profession should not be hindered by setting requirements without relevance to the fitness of, and proper education and training for, its competent practice.
- Continuing professional development should be mandatory, conditioning the renewal of the licence/certificate at periodic intervals, to fostering high levels of competence and conduct.

Anyway:

> Professional regulation cannot, however, be a guarantee against the failure of professional services by individual members, nor can it be a substitute for other mechanisms for redress such as the civil and criminal courts or a substitute for the management of professional staff in the workplace. Rather, it is part of the spectrum of regulatory mechanisms which, taken together, are designed to protect consumers. (Lightman, in Leslie 2013, p. 100)

In sum: As the members of a profession "have the greatest capacity to recognize low standards" (Dingwall 2008, p. 66), then "the social institution of 'delegation and trust' acts to facilitate a collectively rational outcome" (p. 68). When the profession "is perceived to abuse its privileged position, these privileges should be withdrawn. This is ultimately the only workable 'real and effectual discipline'" (p. 76).

Could the teaching profession be self-governing? What can teachers win with it?

References

Bæchler, J. (1994). *Précis de la démocratie*. Paris: Calman-Lévy/Éditions UNESCO.
Competition Bureau. (2007). *Self-regulated professions Balancing competition and regulation*. Ottawa. www.competitionbureau.gc.ca/eic/site/cb-bc.nsf/vwapj/Professions-study-final-E.pdf/$FILE/Professions-study-final-E.pdf
Cox, C., & Foster, S. (1990). *The costs and benefits of occupational regulation*. Bureau of Economics, Federal Trade Commission. Retrieved January 2013 from www.ramblemuse.com/articles/cox_foster.pdf
Damásio, A. (2010). *Self comes to mind: Constructing the conscious brain*. New York: Pantheon Books.
Dingwall, R. (2008). *Essays on professions*. Aldershot: Ashgate.

(Footnote 10 continued)

discipline hearing committees must have at least one public member and that member often chairs the committee.

> Societal expectations with respect to regulatory transparency are achieved in many ways. Meetings of the governing boards of regulatory agencies need to be open to public observation and the public should have access to summaries of the decisions made at each of these meetings. Discipline committee hearings need to be open to the public and the full record of such hearings available on request to the public and the public media. Sufficient public notice of both board and hearing committee meetings needs to be given to the public media and the general public.
> Citizens also expect and deserve the right to get easy access to the disciplinary history of each regulated professional. That is most often accomplished by having such information accessible online via the regulatory organization's website. (p. 5)

Dixon-Woods, M. et al. (2011). Why is UK medicine no longer a self-regulating profession? The role of scandals involving "bad apple" doctors. *Social Science & Medicine*, XXX, 1–8.

Gorman, E. H. (2014). Professional self-regulation in North America: The cases of law and accounting. *Sociology Compass, 8*(5), 491–508.

Kendel, D. (2013). *For the sake of students—A report prepared by Dr. Dennis Kendel on current and future teacher regulation in the province of Saskatchewan.* http://education.gov.sk.ca/educator-services/regulation/for-the-sake-of-students.pdf

Law Reform Commission of Saskatchewan. (2007). *Handbook on professional discipline procedure.* http://lawreformcommission.sk.ca/2007Profdisc1.pdf

Leslie, Ch. (Ed.). (2013). *Towards a royal college of teaching—Raising the status of the profession.* London: The Royal College of Surgeons of England. Retrieved July 2014 from http://filestore.aqa.org.uk/news/pdf/AQA-NEWS-TOWARDS-A-ROYAL-COLLEGE.PDF

MacBeath, J. (2012). *Future of teaching profession.* Education International Research Institute, University of Cambridge—Faculty of Education, Leadership for Learning—The Cambridge Network. http://download.ei-ie.org/Docs/WebDepot/EI%20Study%20on%20the%20Future%20of%20Teaching%20Profession.pdf

McRuer, J. C. (1968–1971). *Report of the royal commission inquiry into civil rights—Report number one.* Toronto: Queens' Printer.

Schultze, R. (2007). What does it mean to be a self-governing regulated profession? *Journal of Property Tax Assessment & Administration, 4*(3), 41–53. Retrieved June 2014 from www.collegeofparamedics.sk.ca/docs/about-us/IPTI-article-on-regulated-professions.pdf

Spada. (2009). *British professions today: The state of the sector.* www.ukipg.org.uk/executive_group_resources/spada-british-professions-today.pdf

Chapter 7
Self-regulation of the Teaching Profession

Abstract The teaching profession's self-regulation already exists in several Anglo-Saxon countries. The general term for its bodies is "Teaching Council". The first one was created in Scotland in 1965, but most now existing were established during the first decade of the twenty-first century. Australia is where they most recently and quickly expanded. The General Teaching Council for Scotland and the Ontario College of Teachers are high profile and have been the most influential in the establishment of other similar bodies, which have varied designations and self-regulatory profiles. In the rest of the world, the regulation of the teaching profession is generally carried out by States, either directly or by means of a special Agency/Authority. If the teaching profession's self-regulation continues to be exceptional worldwide, it is because it meets with resistances, which are chiefly political and/or trade unionist. A strong argument, among others, in favour of it is a matter of fact: it already exists and keeps expanding worldwide. A Charter for Teaching Councils was adopted. In sum: There is no fully true profession without a professional entity —crossing its associative diversity—that should be the *Body* of its unity, the *Face* of its identity, the *Voice* of its authority, the *Guardian* of its integrity and the *Prophet* of its future. In any case, professional self-regulation is not an "Open Sesame", i.e. an automatic solution for all of the teaching profession's problems, let alone of education.

Keywords Teaching council · Resistances · Expansion · Profile

Metaphorically speaking, a profession has its *Body* (expertise), its *Soul* (values) and its *Home* (autonomy), together making its *Honour* (prestige). The teaching profession possesses a great Soul and a growing Body, but does not have its own Home, in most countries being regulated directly by State.

Following MacBeath (2012): "Katzenmeyer and Moller's (2001) reference to 'awakening the sleeping giant of teacher leadership' is an apt metaphor as it captures both the dormant qualities of an underestimated and undervalued profession and the massive potential for leadership lying unexploited" (p. 103). The 2005 OECD study refers to:

© The Author(s) 2015
A. Reis Monteiro, *The Teaching Profession*, SpringerBriefs in Education,
DOI 10.1007/978-3-319-12130-7_7

> ... the development in several countries of Teaching Councils that provide teachers and
> other stakeholder groups with both a forum for policy development and, critically, a
> mechanism for profession-led standard setting and quality assurance in teacher education,
> teacher induction, teacher performance and career development. Such organisations seek to
> obtain for teaching the combination of professional autonomy and public accountability
> that has long characterised other professions such as medicine, engineering and law. This
> would provide teachers with greater input into the criteria for entry to their profession, the
> standards for career advancement, and the basis on which ineffective teachers should leave
> the profession. (p. 216)

Teaching Councils is the general term for the teaching profession's self-governing
bodies that exist in several Anglo-Saxon countries. We are going to see where they
were established, what resistances they encountered and which benefits they are
able to bring. Furthermore, a brief account of the international advancements of
professional self-regulation in the education field is provided.

7.1 Panorama

Regarding the regulation of the teaching profession, two worlds may be
distinguished:

- The Anglo-Saxon world, where the idea of professional self-regulation in the
  education field appeared first in the second half of the nineteenth century,
  inspired by the model of the UK General Medical Council, and having spread to
  other countries and continents later (see Sayer 2000; Willis 2005).
- The rest of the world, where the regulation of the teaching profession is generally carried out by States, either directly or by means of a special Agency/
  Authority.

The first teaching profession's self-governing body was created in 1965—the
General Teaching Council for Scotland—but most now existing were established
during the first decade of the twenty-first century. Australia is where they most
recently and quickly expanded. All the Australian States (except for the little
Norfolk Island) have professional self-governing bodies. Their establishment was
recommended by successive studies and reports. For example, in 2000, the Report
Quality Matters—Revitalising teaching: Critical times, critical choices was published, on the teaching profession's education, prepared by Gregor Ramsey for the
Ministry of Education and Training of New South Wales (the most populous
Australian State). The Report recalled that, in spite of more than twenty studies
having been conducted on the teaching profession during the preceding two decades, the profession kept declining. In this regard, an Australian Parliament Report
(1998) was recalled, as well as the above-mentioned 1997 Report of the Joint ILO/

UNESCO Committee of Experts on the Application of the Recommendation concerning the Status of Teachers (1966).[1] According to the Ramsey (2000) Report:

> Contributors to the Review linked the declining status of teaching to the failure to establish the self-regulatory mechanisms so prominent in many other professions. [...]
> Increasingly, professions are moving toward a social contract model emphasising a commitment to client service in return for the privilege of self-regulation. Such a model requires a code of ethics to govern the practice of the profession's members. (pp. 32, 95)

Taking up a Recommendation of the 1998 Australian Parliament Report, Ramsey's first Recommendation was the following: "That the New South Wales Government establish an Institute of Teachers whose primary purpose is to enhance the level of professionalism of teachers and teaching" (p. 215). It should be endowed with the following powers and functions:

- Adoption of Professional Standards
- Professional accreditation/disaccreditation
- Endorsing/disendorsing courses and programmes of teacher education
- Accreditation of entities involved in providing teacher education
- Advising universities and Government on matters related to the profession
- Promoting the profession's status
- Communication on professional issues among members

The Recommendation was implemented in 2004, when the New South Wales Institute of Teachers was established. In the same year, similar bodies were established in two other Australian States, followed by two more the next year.

At present, there are self-governing bodies for the education professions in the UK, Ireland, Malta, Canada, Australia, New Zealand, South Africa, Thailand, Nigeria, Jamaica, and Fiji Islands, with varying denominations.

- In the UK, there are the GTCS (1965), the General Teaching Council for Wales (GTCW, 1998) and the General Teaching Council for Northern Ireland (GTCNI, 1998).
- In Ireland, there is the Teaching Council of Ireland (TCI, 2006).
- In Canada, there is the Ontario College of Teachers (OCT, 1996).[2]
- In Australia, there are the Teachers Registration Board Tasmania (TRBT, 2000), the Victorian Institute of Teaching (VIT, 2001), the Teachers Registration Board of South Australia (TRBSA, 2004), the Western Australian College of Teaching (WACT, 2004), the New South Wales Institute of Teachers (NSWIT, 2004), the Teacher Registration Board of the Northern Territory (TRBNT, 2005), the

---

[1] www.ilo.org/wcmsp5/groups/public/—ed_dialogue/—sector/documents/meetingdocument/wcms_162259.pdf.

[2] In Ontario, there is also the College of Early Childhood Educators (CECE, 2007).

Queensland College of Teachers (QCT, 2005), the ACP (Australian Capital Territory) Teacher Quality Institute (TQI, 2010).[3]

- In New Zealand, there is the New Zealand Teachers Council (NZTC, 2001).
- In the Fiji Islands, there is the Fiji Teachers Registration Board (FTRB, 2008).
- In Thailand, there is the Teachers Council of Thailand (TCT, 2003).
- In South Africa, there is the South African Council for Educators (SACE, 2001).
- In Nigeria, there is the Teachers Registration Council of Nigeria (TRCN, 1993).
- In Malta, there is the Council for the Teaching Profession (CTPM, 2008).
- In Jamaica, there is the Jamaica Teaching Council (JTC, 2009).

In Hong Kong, the establishment of a General Teaching Council (GTC) was recommended in 1990 by a Committee of the Education Department and continues to be at the top of the agenda of the Council on Professional Conduct in Education created in 1994, which is partly elected and partly appointed.[4]

In the USA, the practice of the teaching profession requires certification or licence issued by a competent body in each State, with varying denominations: Certification Office, Teacher Certification, Teacher Licensure, Teacher Licensing, Teacher Education and Certification, Teacher Education and Licensing, etc. In some of the American States, there have been developments towards conferring more autonomy, professional and public representativeness and powers on the regulatory bodies. For example, the powers conferred on the Hawaii Teacher Standards Board (HTSB), created in 1995, aim "to accord the teaching profession a status comparable to that of other professions" (Amendments to Hawaii Administrative Rules—Title 8—Department of Education, Section 8-54-2).[5] An HTSB booklet (2013)[6] reads:

> The Hawaii Teacher Standards Board was created to enable educators to become a self-regulating profession and to adopt high standards for preparation and licensure. [...] A hallmark of a profession is for the profession to regulate itself, and an independent standards board serves that purpose. [...]
> The National Commission on Teaching and America's Future (NCTAF) considers independent professional standards boards to be critical to maintaining consistent standards that are "not vulnerable to constantly changing politics". Nationally, there are thirteen independent standards boards which collectively license over 670,000 educators and approve 278 preparation programs. HTSB is a member of the National Independent Educator Standards Boards Association (NIESBA).

The GTCS (1965) and the OCT (1996) are high profile and have been the most influential in the establishment of other similar bodies, which have varied self-

---

[3] The Australasian Teacher Regulatory Authorities (ATRA) was established in 2008 by the teacher registration and accreditation authorities to facilitating cooperation and collaboration across the Australian and New Zealand jurisdictions in the regulation of the teaching profession.

[4] See: www.edb.gov.hk/en/about-edb/press/consultation/general-teaching-council/cover.html.

[5] Retrieved July 2014 from www.htsb.org/wp-content/uploads/2012/10/Admin_Rules.pdf.

[6] www.htsb.org/wp-content/uploads/2012/10/HTSB-Booklet-2_2013.pdf.

regulatory profiles. One may distinguish five self-regulatory profile levels: high profile, medium-high profile, medium-low profile, low profile and very low profile.

The conclusions of the reviews of these bodies' performance have been globally positive, sometimes recommending increasing their powers and functions. For example, the GTCS, after a public consultation launched in 2009, became a fully independent body on 2 April 2012.[7]

The Government in Northern Ireland is following the Scottish pathway. The Department for Employment and Learning and the Department of Education launched, between October 2012 and January 2013, a joint consultation on the powers of the GTCNI. The consultation proposed:

- the introduction of new legislation to provide independent status for the Council;
- an extension of its remit to include the registration of Further Education (FE) lecturers; and
- the widening of its disciplinary powers.

Following the "Joint Departmental Response to Consultation—Proposals to Widen the Powers of the GTCNI and Extend its Remit to Include the Further Education Sector",[8] although a small minority "contended that there was no practical or fruitful need for a teaching council in Northern Ireland and drew attention to the decision of the coalition Government to abolish the General Teaching Council for England", 85 % of the respondents (41, including individuals, unions, universities and other organizations), agreed and made further suggestions (p. 5). As a consequence, the Department of Education, in conjunction with the Department for Employment and Learning, will introduce a Bill seeking to address the consultation's outcomes, according to which most of the current regulatory functions of the Department of Education should be removed in order for the GTCNI to become an independent body entrusted with wider and flexible powers.

> Ministers consider that securing independence and strengthening its regulatory powers are necessary to enhance the credibility of the GTCNI and promote its status within the teaching profession. It is considered that an independent GTCNI is essential in order to provide assurance to learners and parents that an effective professional body is overseeing the conduct and standards of the teaching profession.
> The proposals in the Bill will aim to transform the GTCNI into the independent regulatory voice of school teachers and lecturers, tasked with promoting the highest standards of professional conduct and practice and ensuring that the profession is held in high esteem by teachers, other educationalists and the public. (pp. 10, 11)

In Wales, a change also took place, but with mixed results. The GTCW was reconfigured by the Education (Wales) Act of 2014 that received Royal Assent on 12 May 2014: registration became mandatory for Further Education teachers and for teaching support staff in schools and Further Education, and the Council was

---

[7] www.legislation.gov.uk/ssi/2011/215/contents/made.

[8] www.delni.gov.uk/gtcni-consultation-joint-departmental-response-for-publication-june-2014.pdf.

renamed the Education Workforce Council (from 1 April 2015),[9] but the whole outcome was not satisfactory for the profession.

The Education (Wales) Bill was introduced by the Minister for Education and Skills on 1 July 2013. On 13 September, the GTCW presented a "Submission to Children & Young People Committee" (now Children, Young People and Education Committee[10]) where, while recognizing that the functions of the new body "are very similar to those of the GTCW", regretted "a number of clauses within the Bill which increase government control over its operation". In particular, the Minister should develop the first Code of Professional Conduct and Practice (the most disappointing clause); the Council members were appointed by the Government; the Council could not give advice of its own volition, and teachers and support staff in independent schools were not required to register.

The National Union of Teachers Cymru (NUT Cymru) that represents primary and secondary school members and is the largest teaching union in Wales, while welcoming "the Welsh Government's proposals for a professionally-led regulator to include other education professionals",[11] shared "the concerns outlined by the GTCW regarding the failure to address the anomaly which sees teachers working in private and independent schools being excluded from the requirement to be registered and regulated", and also echoed "the GTCW's position in relation to the role of the Minister".

During the stages of the Bill's passage through the National Assembly for Wales, some amendments were approved. In particular, the Council's main functions include the following: "to provide advice on matters related to the persons it regulates and teaching and learning" and "publish any advice it gives" but "with the consent of the Welsh Ministers". They also include, as already laid down in the original Bill, the power "to review and revise the code which specifies standards of professional conduct and practice for registered persons". The Education (Wales) Act 2014 also provides for the potential extension of mandatory registration to independent schools in the future.

However, the Council members "are to be appointed by the Welsh Ministers", although it should be secured "that the majority of members of the Council are, or recently have been, registered persons", which should "act as individuals (that is, they are not to act as representatives of any organisation or body to which they may belong, nor any person, organisation or body that nominated them)". The Council Chair is elected from among its membership.

If the teaching profession's self-regulation continues to be exceptional worldwide, it is because it meets with resistances.

---

[9] For the legislative history of this Act, see: www.senedd.assemblywales.org/mgIssueHistoryHome. aspx?IId=7186.

[10] http://dera.ioe.ac.uk/18445/1/GTCW_Submission_to_CYP_Cttee_-_FINALE.pdf.

[11] www.senedd.cynulliadcymru.org/documents/s500001188/CYP4-23-13%20Papur%203%20-% 20NUT%20Cymru.pdf.

7.2 Resistances

The main cause of the resistances to the teaching profession's self-regulation is probably due to the fact of it having developed as a category of public servants. The resistances are chiefly political or trade unionist:

- States, in general, are not easily willing to share the control of a social function so ideologically sensitive and economically fundamental as the teaching profession is.
- Teachers' trade unions may oppose the establishment of professional self-governing bodies moved by a reflex of rejection for being afraid to lose the monopoly of professional representation and to lose members.

Some cases of failure are illustrative of such resistances.

In Canada, in British Columbia (BC), in 1987, the teaching profession was given an opportunity to become the first one in North America to acquire full self-regulatory status, when the British Columbia College of Teachers (BCCT) was established. It met the opposition of the British Columbia Teachers' Federation (BCTF), created in 1917, which lost the privilege of compulsory membership of all teachers. Thereafter, its strategy was Trojan Horse-like, one striving to block the smooth functioning of the BCCT through the election of own candidates to it ("endorsed candidates").

> Teachers in B.C. walked out in protest on April 28, 1987, shutting down every school in the province. They were united in protesting government legislation that introduced a college of teachers: they hadn't asked for a college of teachers, and they didn't want one.
> The BC College of Teachers was an idea introduced by the Social Credit government of the day. At that time there was only one other college of teachers in the world: in Scotland. The BC College of teachers was the first, and remains the only, professional regulatory body in British Columbia that was imposed upon a profession rather than introduced at the request of, and in consultation with, the profession. [...]
> The headline in the *BCTF Newsletter* of April 9, 1987, stated GOV'T ATTACKS BCTF.
> ...What the government attempted to do with the introduction of a college of teachers was threefold:
> 1. To split off the professional elements of the BCTF [...] and make the BCTF solely a bargaining organization with compulsory membership previously granted by statute removed. This was intended to divide teachers and seriously weaken the BCTF.
> 2. To download the costs of teacher certification from government to teachers.
> 3. To submit teachers to yet another level of discipline [...].
> After debating the merits of boycotting the college or participating in the college to neutralize it and limit its scope of activity, the BCTF decided on the latter.[12]

Throughout the years, it succeeded in undermining the College's effectiveness and credibility. In 2004, the Government organized the election of a new body with fewer representatives of the profession, but the solution did not work any better. The BCCT's irreversible degradation prompted the Government to appoint, in

---

[12] BCTF's Executive Director (Ken Novakowski), in *Teacher Newsmagazine*, Vol. 17, No 7, November/December 2004 (http://bctf.ca/publications/NewsmagArticle.aspx?id=7700).

2010, a "Fact Finder" (J. Donald Avison) to report on its status and to make recommendations. His Report *A College Divided: Report of the Fact Finder on the BC College of Teachers*[13] concluded:

1. The BC College of Teachers is not currently regarded as an independent and credible entity. [...]
2. There is significant evidence that the BC Teachers' Federation has, and continues, to intrude upon the capacity of the BC College of Teachers to be properly regarded as an independent entity responsible for the self-regulation of the teaching profession. [...]
6. The Council has lost the confidence of many within the broader educational community and the likelihood that this damage can be repaired is low. As a result, action will be necessary to substantially re-structure the entity, to replace it entirely or to bring the regulatory function back within the jurisdiction of the provincial government. (p. 32)

The Government decided to replace the BCCT with the British Columbia Teachers' Council (BCTC)[14] to restore confidence in the teaching profession. According to the new Teachers Act that entered into force on 9 January 2012,[15] the BCTC is composed of 15 voting members and one non-voting Government representative appointed by the Minister of Education. The 15 members include three teachers nominated by the BCTF, five teachers elected on a regional basis and seven persons appointed by the Minister based on nominations from several entities of the education field. Although the majority of the BCTC members are professionals, it is no longer an independent body but a "Teacher Regulation Branch of the Ministry of Education".

The BCTC's powers are limited to setting standards for teachers' competence, certification and conduct, as well as to approve teacher education programmes. Besides the BCTC, there is a Commissioner, appointed by the Minister, who oversees the Council, and a Disciplinary and Professional Conduct Board, as well as a Director of Certification. The Disciplinary and Professional Conduct Board consists of nine Council members appointed by the Minister, but only four are professionals. Three-member panels (only one member being a teacher) may be formed to hold public disciplinary hearings on issues concerning fitness, competence and conduct, with the power to revoke, suspend, grant or impose conditions on teaching certificates. The decisions of the panels and of the Commissioner are "final and binding", but may be reviewed by an Administrative Tribunal. There is a prescribed Oath of Office for BCTC's Members and Panel Members Regulation.[16] An annual fee continues to be paid, even though it is one-third lesser than the previous fee.

The tactics deployed by the BCTF to undermine the success of the College of Teachers were a classic example of a 'scorched earth policy' sometimes deployed by nations engaged in warfare. The policy is based upon an assumption that it is preferable to utterly destroy all

---

[13] www.bcct.ca/documents/AboutUs/Council/public_report_avison_gov.pdf.

[14] www.bcteacherregulation.ca/AboutUs/Council.aspx.

[15] www.leg.bc.ca/39th4th/1st_read/gov12-1.htm#section9.

[16] www.bclaws.ca/EPLibraries/bclaws_new/document/ID/freeside/239_2011.

of the assets in your own country rather than risk those assets falling into the hands of an enemy. There are no winners in a scorched earth policy. There were no winners in the sequence of events that culminated in teachers coming under complete government regulation in BC. (Kendel 2013, p. 46)

Still in Canada, in Quebec, in 1997, where there were 46 professional self-governing bodies, the *Conseil pédagogique interdisciplinaire du Québec* (CPIQ: Interdisciplinary Pedagogical Council of Quebec), which represented about 14,000 teachers from preschool education to tertiary education (members of 26 professional associations), required the *Office des professions du Québec* (OPQ: Office of the Professions of Quebec)—that is the authority competent to advise the Government on the establishment of professional self-governing bodies—to establish an *Ordre professionnel des enseignantes et enseignants du Québec* (College of Teachers of Quebec). At the time, a survey revealed that about eight out of ten teachers favoured the initiative.

In 2002, the OPQ published its *Avis de l'Office des professions du Québec sur l'opportunité de constituer un ordre professionnel des enseignantes et des enseignants* (Advisory Opinion of the Office of Professions of Quebec on the opportunity of establishing a College of Teachers). In spite of concluding that the teaching profession meets the criteria for being recognized as a profession as set down in the *Code des Professions* (Code of Professions, Chap. IV, Sect. I, para. 25),[17] the OPQ did not consider it "opportune to recommend the establishment of a College of Teachers" because "it does not seem be needed and is refused by a majority" of professionals (p. 6). In fact, the *Fédération des syndicats de l'enseignement* (FSE: Federation of Teachers' Trade Unions) had launched an aggressive campaign against the project, presenting professional self-regulation as a way more to control the profession and impose additional financial charges onto teachers.

In September 2004, following a request of the Ministry of Education presented in 2002, the *Conseil Supérieur de l'Éducation* (CSE: Education Higher Council) published *Un nouveau souffle pour la profession enseignante—Avis au Ministre de l'Éducation* (A new breath for the teaching profession—Advisory Opinion for the Education Minister) that concluded:

> In its description of a professional ideal for the teaching profession, the *Conseil* stressed the importance of involvement by teachers in defining the mechanisms used to govern the profession. The *Conseil* considers that the literature dealing with professionalization clearly indicates that teachers cannot lay claim to professional status unless they are involved in determining the various aspects of their own profession, since involvement is one of the conditions that define a profession. (Conseil Supérieur de l'Éducation, 2004, p. 40)

The CPIQ proposed to the trade unions the joint preparation of a project, but the FSE and the *Centrale des syndicats du Québec* (CSQ: Central/Federation of Trade Unions of Quebec), formed by 14 federations, organized a referendum and 94.7 %

---

[17] www2.publicationsduquebec.gouv.qc.ca/dynamicSearch/telecharge.php?type=2andfile=/C_26/C26.htmandPHPSESSID=36617b2f4fa6d2928dd8ec6f1def1284.

of the respondents opposed the idea. Moreover, a petition against the project, reaching about 40,000 signatures, was addressed to the National Assembly (see Tardif and Gauthier 1999).

In 2011, the new *Coalition avenir Québec* (Coalition for the Future of Quebec) included in its political programme the establishment of an *Ordre professionnel des enseignants* (College of Teachers), if it would be under the purview of the Government (*Engagement 23*).[18]

In England, there was a General Teaching Council for England (GTCE) established by the Teaching and Higher Education Act (1998). In 2010, a new Government decided to abolish it and many other public bodies. Some of its powers and functions were assumed by a new entity beginning on 1 April 2012: it is the Teaching Agency, an executive branch of the Department for Education (DfE).[19] The GTCE failed because it was never highly supported by the trade unions, nor did its performance always match the level of its mandate and responsibilities.

It is a fact that, compared with the principal self-governing professions, the teaching profession has characteristics that are not favourable for its self-regulation. They include the following:

- its scope is diffuse: the aims of education are very broad—the formation of the human personality, whose dimensions are multiple and whose variables are not all controlled by the profession;
- it has an "open professionality" to the extent that its object does not have a mere scientific–technological nature, as it includes moral and political dimensions that are not of the exclusive forum of competence of its professionals;
- its functional content is diversified because, besides instruction, teachers have to perform other roles and to respond to other needs of children, adolescents or youth, even if they are not prepared to do it;
- it is highly heterogeneous, given the diversity of teachers' academic backgrounds, and its different levels of practice in the education system, resulting in intraprofessional cleavage;
- its knowledge base is not so well identified nor is it so uncontroversially specialized as those professions based on knowledge with a different epistemic nature;
- it has a "collective professionalism", because its practice encompasses a typical collective dimension: teachers work principally in classes, and this requires some collective preparation too;
- it is practised mainly under a salaried regime, and teachers have a margin of judgement, decision and responsibility inferior to those of professions with analogous education and relevance;

---

[18] http://coalitionavenirquebec.org/wp-content/uploads/2012/07/Plateforme-20124.pdf.

[19] http://media.education.gov.uk/assets/files/pdf/t/teaching%20agency%20framework%20document.pdf.

- its practice is not deemed to have the potential to cause damages justifying a special protection of their "clients", especially by means of appropriate and enforceable Professional Ethics;
- its professional relationship is not just free, insomuch as school attendance is compulsory and the pupils, in general, cannot choose their teachers nor may teachers refuse pupils;
- the identification of its main "clients"—and of the corresponding professional responsibilities—is somewhat ambiguous: are they students? their parents? school authorities? State?;
- its direct addressees are "minors", in general, and most of them are not very interested in the professional services (a fact that is not favourable to the profession's prestige);
- the traditional predominance of women in the profession is also said to be not favourable to its prestige;
- teachers cannot create the professional distance that is a factor of status of other professions, because the teaching profession's professionalism includes a peculiar dimension of empathy and caring;
- it is frequently accessible to persons that do not possess a minimum or specific education (or are even unsuitable) to practise it, such accessibility being one of the most corrosive factors of its professionality.

Nevertheless, the teaching profession possesses other features comparable to the principal self-governing professions, some of which distinguishing it advantageously. They include the following:

- education is perhaps the most complex and difficult human endeavour (an idea that is recurrent in the history of pedagogic thought);
- education is a human right and a global public good deserving recognized priority;
- the profession provides the most universal service, insofar as school attendance is compulsory;
- it possesses specific theoretical and practical knowledge whose learning requires an education that should be relatively long;
- its autonomy, although inferior to that of other analogous professions, is significant and may be increased;
- the pedagogic relationship is one of the most asymmetric professional relations, in particular when it is about educating children;
- professional wrongs in education have the potential to cause serious damage to the students and the whole society, which may not be immediately perceptible.

The foregoing permits the conclusion that the requirements, the resonance and the responsibility of the teaching profession are not globally inferior to those of the principal self-governing professions and, in some regards, are even superior.

7.3 Benefits

The arguments and benefits of professional self-regulation in the education field may be summarized in the following sentences, which are inevitably somewhat redundant:

1. *The teaching profession is a great profession, but does not have a great professionality.*

David Carr (2000) noted that "medicine, law and education are arguably the 'big three' civilised bulwarks against the time-honoured human curses of pestilence, injustice and ignorance" (p. 45). The teaching profession is recognized worldwide as one of the most important functions in modern societies, being the most universal, fundamental, ethical and personal profession, as justified above. Teachers are perhaps the professionals that spend more time in direct contact with their main "clients", who are principally children, adolescents and youth: several hours a day, 5 days a week, about 40 weeks a year and for many years. They form the largest professional group in most contemporary societies.

Notwithstanding, the teachers' status worldwide is far from acceptable, as shown especially in Sect. 4.1. Their status varies from country to country and is not uniform even within each country, but the decline and lack of recognition of the teaching profession, together with its becoming more and more complex, difficult, demanding and practised in unfavourable or even undignified conditions, all cause many teachers to be ashamed of it, leading to growing attrition and undermining its attractiveness. As the Report of the Parliament of the Commonwealth of Australia (1998) found: "Few teachers recommend a teaching career to their children or their brightest students. Some are even ashamed to admit to being teachers" (p. 11). According to the 1998 UNESCO Report:

> The fact that society still is willing to accept at all that people can be employed as teachers without having received any specific preparation for the job points to the difficulty for teachers in getting their claims heard. Probably no other aspect of teacher employment policies has done as much to retard progress towards recognition of teaching as a profession. (p. 46)

Sayer (2000), after affirming that teachers "have the ingredients of a profession, without the hallmarks", wrote:

> A full profession is one which provides a major and essential public service, which is founded on a body of knowledge and skills for which a long training of high standard is essential, and which exercises a significant measure of responsibility for the service it provides. […]
> Teaching is seen as both a calling and a craft. Its activities are related to generally recognized definitions of a 'profession' […].
> Teachers […] need to have ownership of the teaching task. They need to feel responsible and professionally accountable for the quality of service provided. It may well be, as some sociologists have argued, that profession is a term so variously defined that it is incapable of general definition and of little scientific value. However, it is certainly a symbolic label for a desired status; it is certainly a term which has meaning to people who apply it to

themselves; it has felt reality, and that is a prevalent if not universal feeling among teachers. (pp. 40, 103, 158)

If teachers wish to raise their level of professionality, they have to struggle for it.

2. *Nobody will do for teachers what only they, individually and collectively, can and should do for themselves.*

The teaching profession today possesses an identity, an authority and a responsibility transcending the traditional dependency of its usual practice. It justifies the recognition of its autonomy as a profession and greater independence for its professionals. As Gerard Kelly, Editor of the *Times Education Supplement*, rightly pointed out, referring to the absence of a self-governing body for the teaching profession in England:

> Transient politicians, non-teaching amateurs and opinionated newspaper columnists have filled this void, to the detriment of teachers and the confusion of pupils and parents.
> It doesn't have to be this way. The profession needs a Royal College of Teaching, owned, run and directed by it. Because if teachers do not own their profession, then others with more conflicted intentions surely will. (in Leslie 2013, p. 105)

Indeed, teachers are the ones who know and should do what "politicians and bureaucrats should not and cannot properly exercise", as the press release of the GTC (England and Wales) movement on 16 July 1991 read (as cit. in Sayer 2000, p. 47). During the debate on the Education Bill at the House of Lords, in 1993, Lord Judd said: "The establishment of a GTC, possibly at a stroke, would repair the morale of the teaching profession and reverse the decline in the public perception of teachers" (p. 80). During another session, Lord Dormand of Easington affirmed: "Such a body would not only raise the status of the teaching profession in the eyes of the public and parents; it would raise the standards and the morale of teachers themselves" (p. 72). This was also the standing of the Irish National Teachers' Organization (1992):

> Therefore, a radical new approach to teacher professionalism is required in order to enhance the professional status of teachers, one which entails teachers themselves asserting greater control over their enterprise and seeking State approval for greater self-regulatory control. [...]
> In particular, they must forge a professionalism distinctively suited to the basic values of their own enterprises, one which involves promoting a caring concern for the child as client, resisting external interference in the pupil/teacher relationship, establishing confidence and trust in the education system and in the competence of teachers to deliver a high quality education service. [...]
> Teachers must rightly impose their own personal blueprint upon professionalism, a professionalism which involves assuming greater occupational control and increased professional responsibility at school and at national level. It also entails building a new sense of idealism in teaching where every effort to ennoble the art of teaching is encouraged and supported. Teachers must also become the authoritative voice in education.
> It is clear that State regulated control fosters dependence upon the State rather than independence and autonomy. Teachers must, therefore, be empowered to break away from an over reliance upon the State and its various agencies. In order to ensure that the highest

professional ideals are encouraged and maintained, teachers must vigorously pursue the
establishment of An Chomhairle Mhuinteolreachta [Teaching Council]. (pp. 34, 36)

In short: Who should know better and be more interested than teachers in caring
about their profession, for the benefit of education too?

3. *It is in the interest of education and of the profession to distinguish both
   between governmental and professional responsibilities, as well as between
   strict labour issues and more general professional matters.*

If the status of the teaching profession is as it is in so many countries, it is because
neither its administrative direct regulation has been up to the level of its demands
and responsibilities, nor have its professional associations cared well enough for it.

On the one hand, when most teachers are public servants, there is a conflict of
interests between the position of the State as employer and its functions as regulator
of the profession that may affect the credibility and the confidence it should deserve
from the professionals and public opinion.

[G]overnments' core responsibilities in education should be described in terms of the
quality of the resources and the working conditions in schools. [...] It is up to the profession, however, to specify the standards that should apply to teaching practice. (Parliament of the Commonwealth of Australia 1998, p. 13)

On the other hand, the perception of trade unions being most concerned with "bread
and butter" issues does not favour their credibility and the confidence their positions
and proposals should deserve from public opinion when professional issues more
directly related to the quality of education are at stake. This was remarked in 1955,
at the Assembly of Delegates of the World Confederation of Organizations of the
Teaching Profession (WCOTP), meeting in Istanbul, having as theme "Status of the
Teaching Profession". George Ashbridge, a member of the WCOTP Executive,
said:

It may be that in the immediate future the success of our teacher organizations in raising the
status of teachers – in the comprehensive sense of the term – will depend on our ability to
reconcile our trade union functions (salaries, conditions of employment, legal protection of
members, and so forth) with our strictly professional functions (raising the quality of the
service teachers give). There can be real conflict here between loyalty to the individual
member who has paid his dues and loyalty to the teaching service as a whole and to the
children we serve. (as cit. in Towsley, 1991, p. 6)

Also following an OECD Report (2011a), "issues of collective bargaining can be
successfully separated from professional issues, where teachers and their organizations collaborate with ministry staff in self-governing bodies to oversee work on
entry, discipline, and the professional development of teachers" (p. 56).

That is what distinguishes a professional self-governing body from an associative one, such as a trade union or another professional association. Trade unions are
essentially organizations for the advancement of the economic–labour interests and
welfare of their members. On the contrary, while professional self-governing bodies
may act on promoting their professions and give voice to their best interests, the
principle of their legitimacy and responsibility is the primacy of the public interest.

That is also why the dual role of several Canadian professional associations that function both as unions and as self-regulatory bodies arouses an inherent conflict of interests, because advocacy functions (bargaining) and regulatory functions (serving the public interest) are hardly compatible. They should be allocated to different organizations, as the Supreme Court of Canada decided in 1973, in a case concerning the Saskatchewan Registered Nurses Association.

4. *A teaching profession self-governing body does not compete with the duties of the public power concerning the right to education or with trade unions' functions regarding the protection of the interests of their membership.*

In democratic Rule of Law, the basis of both political legitimacy and professional legitimacy with respect to education is the same: it is the normative content of the universal human right to education, as internationally agreed. The teaching profession's self-regulation is subsidiary to the obligations of States for respecting, protecting and fulfilling the right to education. If they do not comply with their international and often constitutional obligations, teachers remain subject to their professional ethical duties. They have the right and the obligation to question education policies not respecting the integrity of the right to education. In this regard, Meryl Thompson (1997) stressed the fact that:

> The concept of acting independently with integrity on behalf of the client and, if necessary, being critical is an essential element of professionalism. [...] Teachers as a body are right to question policy on the basis of educational research and the pedagogic knowledge of teachers and to try to influence debate. (pp. 55, 57)

Besides the ethical–legal legitimacy based on the right to education and the epistemological legitimacy based on the specific expertise of the teaching profession, there is the personal legitimacy of their professionals when they distinguish themselves for their personal, ethical, intellectual and civic excellence.

The teaching profession's self-regulation does not compete with the trade unions' functions either. Teachers' professionalism and unionism are not opposed. Their legitimacy and purpose are different, as above mentioned, but complementary.

- A trade union is a Private Law institution, whose legal basis is the freedom of association, having as its main purpose the protection and promotion of the economic-labour interests of its membership.
- A professional self-governing body is, in general, a Public Law institution, whose legal basis is a statute endowing it with powers and functions concerning the regulation of a profession for the protection of the public interest.

The priority of the public interest finds expression in the primacy of general professional matters, concerning the competence and conduct of its membership, over the strictly trade unionist ones. However, the two may and should collaborate. As the Irish Minister for Education and Science stressed, by presenting at the Parliament the Teaching Council Bill (2000)[20] on 24 October 2000:

---

[20]   http://debates.oireachtas.ie/dail/2000/10/24/00015.asp.

The role of the Teaching Council in representing teachers is distinct from the role of the teacher unions. While there are many areas of common interest to the Teaching Council and the teacher unions, there is a fundamental difference between their roles. The Teaching Council will be concerned with promoting and maintaining the highest standards within the teaching profession. Negotiations on conditions of service, salaries and pensions will remain the preserve of the teaching unions. There is no contradiction in this arrangement; the work of the two bodies will complement each other.

Also, the Irish National Teachers' Organization (1992) pointed out:

Under State regulation the activities of teacher unions are likely to be perceived as more important than the pursuit of professional associations. The teacher unions already provide protection in relation to salaries and conditions of service, indicating perhaps that teachers perceive that they have more important interests to defend than the label applied to status distinctions. The lack of urgency in pursuing the enactment of An Chomhairle Mhuln-teoireachta – a Teaching Council is due to a degree of ambiguity, uncertainty and lack of a clear appreciation amongst the various teacher organisations regarding the value of self-regulatory control. The fact that other professionals working within bureaucratic institutions, most notably members of the medical profession, are increasingly turning to trade union activities to improve their conditions of service highlights the need to maintain a strong trade union presence alongside a professional organisation. There is no apparent reason why both cannot coexist in harmony with each other. There is no reason, furthermore, why both institutional arrangements could not complement one another in their attempts to enhance teacher status and to increase their power relationships *vis-à-vis* the State and other groups. (pp. 17, 18)

Professional self-governing bodies, therefore, do not invade the trade unions' space, but rather expand it by instituting a new instance of professional intervention open to trade unionist participation.

5. *A professional self-regulation body is a superior authority for participation and decision-making regarding questions central to the profession and to education.*

Although the public mandate of a teaching profession's self-governing body excludes both strictly political and strictly trade unionist issues, it should not be indifferent to any matter concerning its professionals and education. In this respect, Michael Sexton (2007) wrote:

Above all else, teachers must be willing to engage with the 'bigger issues' – the moral, political, social and philosophical issues that one way or another form the backdrop to the more practical considerations that make up the common daily experience of teachers' working lives. More than any other professional group, teachers can act as agents for the creation of a better society, and they should not shy away from this role. If they have the courage and confidence to take on this role […] almost inevitably the status of the teaching profession will be raised. To achieve this, it is imperative that teachers be proactive in seeking to involve themselves in the shaping of educational policy rather than merely implementing it and, given its remit to represent the teaching profession on educational issues, the Teaching Council is the body best placed to do this. (p. 96)

A teaching profession's self-governing body with a composition representative of the profession but also of the public interest (including representatives of the Ministry) and other legitimate interests in the education field (such as families and professional education institutions)—so that no one interest group has undue influence on it—is a forum for uniting political with professional legitimacy, fused in Professional Standards. In the 2013 Teaching Profession Summit:

> Participants agreed that for teaching standards to be credible to the profession and perceived as fair, teachers must have a lead role in developing them. [...] Professions are characterized by a body of knowledge, a moral commitment to their clients, and standards of practice that are developed by the profession. (Asia Society 2013, pp. 10, 11)

A self-governing body is the most appropriate authority, in particular, for promoting the adoption of and supervising compliance with, a Professional Ethics that is a cornerstone of higher professionality. As the ILO *Handbook* (2012) remarks: "The authority set up to promote and apply codes of conduct and associated disciplinary procedures varies by country, from administrative authorities to voluntary or mandatory professional bodies, but the concept of a teaching council or equivalent is increasingly adhered to in many countries" (p. 105). This is acknowledged by the EI "Resolution on the Future of the Teaching Profession", adopted in 2011 at its 6th World Congress (Cape Town, South Africa), that affirms: "Where professional teaching councils are established on a national basis, teachers should be at the centre of deciding the nature and remit of those councils" (u).[21]

6. *The teaching profession's self-regulation means an appropriation of powers that are no longer exercised by supervisory authorities but turn into being exercised "inter pares".*

When there is a governmental Agency/Authority to regulate the teaching profession, professionals are co-opted to do it. These professionals possess a political legitimacy (derived from appointment) and may possess personal legitimacy (based on their individual merit), but they lack the professional legitimacy only the profession possesses when it is self-governing.

Studies on the attitude of teachers regarding the possibility of the establishment of a professional self-governing body reveal that the main objections of the most resistant include the following:

- Professional Standards can be an instrument for added control of teachers' work, rather than for the enhancement of their status.
- Professional discipline can give rise to abuses and arbitrariness, both by school authorities and by the public, in particular families.

While deviations from the *raison d'être* of professional self-regulation are always possible, they may be prevented, and one should not lose sight of the essential point: The primacy of the public interest, underlying the self-regulation statute, demands that a professional self-governing body assumes as its principal mission that of caring for the professionalism of its members.

Consequently, it is not the case that a teaching profession's self-governing body is one more instance of power over teachers; it is, rather, a power they win. They should not be afraid of Professional Standards adopted by the profession itself, or

---

[21] http://pages.ei-ie.org/library/en/libraries/detail/159.

fear the disciplinary power exerted by a professional self-governing body. While the main purpose of the Standards is the protection of the interests of children, adolescents, youth and the society in general, they also serve to protect teachers from unacceptable interferences in their competences and responsibilities, on the part of the school authorities and on the part of families, as well as from frivolous complaints. Exerting disciplinary power is, furthermore, both an obligation and a right:

- It is an obligation resulting from the principle of the primacy of the public interest that implies sanctioning professional incompetence and misconduct.
- It is a right as well because sanction for breaches of Professional Standards is also in the interest of the profession, which should be able to protect itself from the behaviour of its members that may affect its dignity, honour and prestige.

Another objection may be that of having to pay membership fees, but that is a duty common to all self-governing professions. Budgetary independence is a factor of functional autonomy. One might also say in this case that freedom has a price.[22]

7. *Professional self-regulation is a privilege the teaching profession should want and deserve to have.*

Professions' regulation is a right and an obligation of States, as recalled earlier. Therefore, self-regulation is not a right the teaching profession may claim but, rather, a privilege to which it may aspire and that should deserved by taking on the corresponding responsibility. It is as follows:

- the privilege of assessing the suitability of a person to hold the professional title, that is, of certifying/licensing and disciplining the members of the profession, supported by the powers of law-making and enforcing rules and by-laws over the professional membership; and
- the responsibility of exercising the self-regulatory powers and functions giving priority to the interests of the profession's clients and to the public interest in

---

[22] James Casey, the author of a reference study (*The Regulation of Professions in Canada*, 1994), commented:

> Someone once said it is every Canadian's God-given and inalienable right to complain about the boss. It also appears to be every professional's right to complain about the fees they are required to pay.
> The many tasks currently performed by professional bodies require a significant level of financial resources, most of which must come directly from the members. This is as it should be. Strong financial support assists in building a strong profession, and a strong profession is in the members' best long-term interests. Most importantly, a strong profession helps further and protect the public interest. One of the primary advantages of self-governance is that the profession has the ability to control its own destiny. A weak profession that is unable to adequately fulfil its responsibilities may lose the privilege of self-governance.
> (Retrieved January 2013 from www.cap.ab.ca/pdfs/selfgovprofchall.pdf).

general, if needed taking disciplinary action against practitioners in breach of the Professional Standards.

Consequently: "Professionality demands that trust exist between the teachers and the general public, and this is achieved by showing that teachers are committed to the maintenance of high standards" (Irish National Teachers' Organization 1994, p. 40). In this respect, Ramsey (2000) observed: "The community bestows on the profession the responsibility and privilege of self-regulation, and in return the profession fulfils the obligations of its social contract" (p. 125). The Standards for the Education, Competence and Professional Conduct of Educators in British Columbia[23] read:

> Professionals enter into a contract with the public that provides the professionals with a level of autonomy and self-regulation in return for an agreement that the profession will place the interests of the public above individual interests. Professionals agree to be accountable to the public, and the Standards serve as a touchstone for this responsibility.

Ivor Sutherland, former GTCS Registrar, asked: "What can be more important for the teaching profession than the opportunity to take command of its own professional affairs and control of its own destiny?" (as cit. in Van Nuland 1998, p. 182).

8. *With self-regulation, teachers gain a profession.*

Professional self-regulation is an added value to the teaching profession, protecting its title. For example, like Ontario's other regulated professions, the Ontario College of Teachers adopted, in 2008, the designation Ontario Certified Teacher (OCT or EAO in French: Enseignant/e Agréé/e de l'Ontario). Only certified College members in good standing have the right to use OCT on letterhead, business cards and professional materials.

Becky Francis, Director of the Academies Commission, of the Pearson Think Tank, and Professor of Education and Social Justice at King's College London, highlighted this fact:

> Teaching as a profession is unique. It is made up of experts in every subject imaginable who are simultaneously expert in the science of pedagogy and skilled in the art of teaching. Teachers can be found in formal and non-formal settings in schools, colleges, universities, hospitals, businesses, factories, homes, military establishments and youth groups. In no other profession do the practitioners come from such a wide variety of backgrounds or practise in such a wide variety of settings with such a wide variety of qualifications and training.
> And yet, unlike other professions, teaching has no single body which independently represents, pulls together and supports the development of the myriad professionals and organisations that work to support them. Such a body is vital for the long-term growth, health and independence of a profession. (in Leslie 2013, p. 108)

When there is a constellation of professional associations, their representativeness and functions are partial: each one represents only its associates and has objectives

---

[23] www.bcteacherregulation.ca/documents/AboutUs/Standards/edu_stds.pdf.

focused on the defence of certain interests, and divergence and competition may sometimes arise.

That is why the establishment of a self-governing body was struggled for and welcomed by teaching profession associations in general, including trade unions. For example, in Ireland, the Secretary General of Irish National Teachers' Organisation (INTO) wrote in the Preface to *The Teaching Council Act 2001—Question and Answer Guide*, published in 2004: "I urge all members to take an active interest in the development of the Council, the establishment of which has been an INTO objective for decades".[24] According to Deborah Lawson, Secretary General of the UK Union for Education Professionals (Voice):

> Morale within teaching is at a low point because of a lack of esteem within the profession and a decline in government and public respect for teachers. We would welcome any attempt to raise the status of teaching as a profession and restore public confidence and respect.
>
> We had hoped that the General Teaching Council for England (GTC) would rise to this challenge. […]
>
> An examination of GTC's failure is crucial in ensuring that any Royal College of Teaching is correctly founded.
>
> It should be independent of government, owned and controlled by teachers, and open to teachers in all phases of education (nursery to tertiary) in both the public and private sectors. (in Leslie 2013, p. 74)

In the opinion of Brian Lightman, Secretary General of the UK Association of School and College Leaders (ASCL):

> The greatest challenge will be to win the hearts and minds of the teaching profession, who have an enormous amount to gain from having their own professional body. This would enhance their professional status by setting out a sustainable, long-term vision for the development of the profession and would provide them with a much-needed cushion from short term political considerations driven by the electoral cycle.
>
> The time is now right for this idea to be debated by the profession. (ib. p. 79)

In sum: There is no fully true profession without a professional entity—crossing its associative diversity—that should be the:

- *Body* of its unity
- *Face* of its identity
- *Voice* of its authority
- *Guardian* of its integrity
- *Prophet* of its future

A strong argument in favour of the teaching profession's self-regulation is thus a matter of fact: it already exists and works.

---

[24] www.into.ie/ROI/Publications/TeachingCouncilAct01QA.pdf.

7.4 Expansion

The movement towards the establishment of self-governing bodies for the teaching profession keeps expanding.

In Canada, as we saw, while self-regulation is the gold standard of professional regulation, there is currently only a self-governing body of the teaching profession, in Ontario (OCT, 1997), after the failure of the BCCT, established in 1987 but dissolved in 2012. In other Canadian provinces/territories, teachers' certification is regulated only by Governments, but their professional misconduct is jointly regulated with the Teacher Associations in Alberta, Saskatchewan and Manitoba. Also noteworthy is the fact that mandatory teacher membership in a provincial teachers' association or federation became universal across Canada by the 1960s, a privilege that prompted them to lobby Governments to grant them professional regulatory powers.

> By the mid-1990s, as the emphasis on accountability escalated throughout Canada, several provincial governments had begun to explore the possibility of splitting unitary teacher organizations into two entities in order to separate their activities which were perceived to create a conflict of interest. Some governments proposed the creation of a college of teachers with mandatory membership, charged with teacher certification, professional development, disciplinary matters and the assurance of competency. A second organizational body would then have voluntary membership and concentrate upon collective bargaining and teacher welfare. From the perspective of government, this option seemed like a plausible vehicle by which to make the teaching profession completely self-regulated. However, others saw it as an attempt to divide and diminish the power of teacher organizations and transfer the regulatory costs to teachers. (Saskatchewan Teachers' Federation 2013, p. 8)

This is the case in Saskatchewan, when teachers are certified through the Ministry of Education, but the discipline of the profession is mainly handled by the Saskatchewan Teachers' Federation (STF), established in 1935. *The Teachers' Federation Act*, amended in 1948, in 1970 and in 1997, gives the STF powers concerning the conduct of its members. The STF thus holds a dual role as the advocate for teachers' economic-labour interests and the protector of the public from professional incompetence or misconduct on the part of teachers. However, the Saskatchewan Government retains complete regulatory power over Superintendents and Directors of Education, which are not STF members (but schools' Principals are), and another subset of teachers (in independent schools and schools on reserves) who are not STF members either. Teachers are thus regulated under three different regimes.

In August 2013, the Ministry of Education decided to commanded a study to provide recommendations to address concerns regarding the regulation of the teaching profession. The position taken by the STF, while recognizing "that professionally led regulation is a privilege, not a right", in a democratic society, and in spite of concluding that "there is little justification for the unilateral imposition of an alternative model of professional regulation" (Saskatchewan Teachers' Federation 2013, pp. 12, 18), was rather cautious and moderate:

A principled and robust system of self-regulation is not only in the public interest, it also raises the status of the teaching profession. […]
The Saskatchewan Teachers' Federation understands that the current review of teacher regulation in our province may result in recommendations to establish an alternative framework requiring legislative changes to *The Education Act, 1995, The Teachers' Federation Act, 2006* and *The League of Educational Administrators, Directors and Superintendents Act, 1991.* If so, it is very important that the foundation of any new structures and systems is built with care, be professionally led, and involve all educational stakeholders including students, parents and the public to ensure success. […]
Regardless of when legislative changes are introduced by the Government of Saskatchewan, there will be a period of time when existing disciplinary systems will continue to serve the public interest. To bolster confidence in that part of the system over which it has authority, the STF is committed to implementing immediate administrative changes. (pp. 1, 13, 16)

The study commanded by the Government (Kendel 2013), while recognizing that the "proposed administrative changes are commendable and should be implemented as expeditiously as possible" by the STF, affirmed that "those changes alone will not be sufficient to remedy the current fragmentation of teacher regulation and the inescapable conflicts of interest inherent in a unitary model in which professional advocacy and collective bargaining coexist with public protection in a single organization" (p. 82). In the author's opinion: "The current regulatory fragmentation that is inherent in having teachers regulated under three separate statutes can only be resolved by consolidating regulation for all teachers under the authority of a single organization". It considered three alternatives/models:

One of the models I considered is the current arrangement in which authority and responsibility for teacher regulation is divided between the STF and the provincial Government. For ease of reference, I call this the 'divided' model.
The second model is one in which all authority and responsibility for teacher regulation is held by the Government of Saskatchewan and administered through its Ministry of Education. I call this the 'government' model.
The third model is one in which all authority and responsibility for teacher regulation would be entrusted to the teaching profession through a statute that establishes an agency dedicated exclusively to teacher regulation. Because such agencies in BC and Ontario were called Colleges of Teachers, I call this the 'college' model. (p. 72)

The Kendel Report concluded:

I cannot endorse any model that leaves the public protection roles and teacher advocacy roles in a single organization […].
I believe that creating a Saskatchewan College of Teachers modelled upon the 17 year history of a very successful Ontario College of Teachers would best serve the interests of students and parents in this province. […]
If the teaching profession in Saskatchewan is not prepared to support regulation through a College of Teachers, with considerable regret, I would recommend regulation by the Ministry of Education as the alternative option. […]
In summary, I can only endorse a College of Teachers model and a Ministry of Education model as future models for teacher regulation in Saskatchewan. I regard a College of Teachers model as highly preferable for two reasons. First, I believe this model would most effectively serve and protect the interests of students and parents. Secondly, I believe this

model offers teachers in the Saskatchewan the opportunity they deserve to exercise full responsibility and accountability for regulation of their profession. (pp. 83, 84, 85)

One of his five recommendations to the Government of Saskatchewan was as follows: "I recommend that the Government of Saskatchewan organize a visit to the Ontario College of Teachers by a delegation which includes education sector leaders from Saskatchewan as well as some students and parents to determine the factors contributing to the success of that regulatory model and apply those lessons in Saskatchewan" (Recommendation 4) (p. 88).

Based on the Kendel Report, the Ministry of Education announced that a new body will be established, exclusively devoted to the regulation of the teaching profession. The transition is expected to be complete by October 2015.

In England, there was a General Teaching Council for England, as above mentioned. The 2012 Report of the Education Committee of the House of Commons *Great teachers: attracting, training and retaining the best—Ninth Report of Session 2010–2012, Volume I: Report, together with formal minutes* read:

> 20. We acknowledge and support the case for a new, member-driven College of Teaching, independent from but working with Government, which could play important roles, inter alia, in the accreditation of CPD [Continuing Professional Development] and teacher standards. We are not convinced that the model of 'Chartered Teacher' status proposed by the existing College of Teachers will bring about the changes required to teachers' CPD and career progression opportunities, or that the existing College has the public profile or capacity to implement such a scheme. We recommend that the Government work with teachers and others to develop proposals for a new College of Teaching, along the lines of the Royal Colleges and Chartered Institutions in other professions. (para. 114) (p. 53)

In the wake of this Report, on 5 September 2012, in the Prince's Teaching Institute, in London, a meeting took place to discuss the idea of establishing a new autonomous professional body, perhaps a Royal College like other professions have (nineteen in all). It gathered representatives of various education sectors, such as trade unions and other professional associations, the Education International, the Institute of Education of London and Faculty of Education of Cambridge and of other universities. According to the meeting report, after the abolition of the GTCE, there was a general feeling of a lack in the profession of a common voice with authority to speak, not only for the teachers but also for the profession too, and to project and cultivate its ideal. To pave the way towards the establishment of a new self-governing body, it was decided to set up a Committee of teachers formed by participants in the meeting, under the coordination of the Prince's Teaching Institute. A Commission of senior individuals was also created to explore the idea.

In June 2013, the Committee and the Commission authored a Discussion Document that evolved into a blueprint published in February 2014, after an extensive consultation and broad debates within the education community.[25] According to the blueprint:

---

[25] The blueprint and further information and documents on this process may be found at www.princes-ti.org.uk/CollegeofTeaching.

> This is an idea whose time has come. A new College of Teaching has the potential to become the deeply respected voice on professional matters that teaching needs, and to develop the teaching profession in this country as the finest in the world. In doing so, we believe that it will make a significant contribution to the lives and life chances of children and young people in this and future generations and so to the success of our country. (p. 4)

The College of Teaching, as envisaged, will not be a regulatory body with mandatory membership and disciplinary power. Its principal activities would be:

1. Setting standards,
2. Enhancing professionals' development,
3. Informing professional practice, standards and policy with evidence (p. 6).

The successor of the GTCE is work in progress.

In the Caribbe, the Caribbean Community (CARICOM), composed of 15 member and 5 associated States, set up in 2006 an Advisory Committee for education quality affairs. In 2007, a Task Force on Teaching and Teacher Education for preparing a CARICOM Council for Teaching and Teacher Education (CCCTTE) that will supervise the functioning of National Teaching Councils was established. The Task Force prepared a Draft Document to Establish National Councils and a Draft Professional and Academic Standards for Teachers that were discussed at regional and national levels, since 2010, with the support and participation of the Caribbean Union of Teachers.[26] As the document "Regional Standards of Practice for the Teaching Profession—Draft Framework of Generic Teaching Performance Standards and Academic Standards (1th Revision)"[27] reads, the Standards keep "with international trends and good practices" and "are intended to guide the work of the National Teaching Council, or its counterpart, as it prepares to fulfill its mandate as the voice of the teaching profession".

> With a mandate to regulate the teaching profession, the National Council for Teaching and Teacher Education (NCTTE) or its counterpart, in each member state, will be the responsible body for maintaining standards through the registration and licensing process. The act of licensing an education professional is an acceptance that such a person is competent to work in the field of education in the CARICOM region.

Consequently:

> It is important that those who will be most affected by the proposals understand and appreciate the inherent value in having a well regulated teaching profession. The measures that will be eventually introduced are meant to facilitate, nurture and support teacher development, and thereby enhance quality assurance and the status of the profession. In no way should they be interpreted as punitive or threatening.

In April 2013, the Caribbean Community Task Force for Teacher Education submitted "Standards of Practice for the Teaching Profession in the Caribbean Community—Draft Framework of Generic Teaching Performance Standards and

---

[26] www.caricom.org/jsp/pressreleases/pres419_10.jsp.

[27] http://community.oas.org/iten_ried/iten/f/1030/p/3229/4395.aspx#4395.

Academic Standards".[28] It reads: "This document presents the final draft standards framework that has been developed for the region. It is the outcome of several revisions that have resulted from widespread consultations among key stakeholders across the region" (Preface).

> The Task Force continues to encourage countries either to establish National Councils for Teaching and Teacher Education (NCTTE) or to examine their present institutions to determine how they could be upgraded to carry out the work of the National Council, while working towards the establishment of the Caribbean Community Council for Teaching and Teacher Education. (p. 8)

In India, a Commission appointed by the National Council for Teacher Education (NCTE), in June 2010, for preparing a draft Code of Professional Ethics of Teachers, wrote in its Report delivered in October of the same year: "Like all other professions, the teaching profession should also move towards self-regulation".[29]

The idea of developing teacher professionalism in Europe via extending professionally led regulation is also advancing.

In the Netherlands, the Ministry of Education, Culture and Science launched a Teachers Agenda 2013–2020, developed in consultation with teachers and teacher educators, among others. It includes the establishment of "A strong professional association".[30]

In Austria, in 2005, the Ministry of Education commanded a group of experts to study issues of teaching professionality and professionalization, within the context of increasing internationalization of education, which should include the development of guidelines for the future. The Working Group name was *Entwicklung von Professionalität im Internationalen Kontext* (Development of the Professionality within the International Context). The study was published in 2011. In his personal contribution, the Group's President (Michael Schratz) dedicates some pages to the Ontario College of Teachers and concludes:

> The Ontario College of Teachers is a good example of how the profession profile and recognition may be improved if it owns a professional organization to assume the responsibility for its professionality, concerned with its quality both at the internal and external levels. [...] The establishment of such an entity could, in the German speaking countries too, give new impetus to professionalization and influence the development of the teaching profession quality. (Schratz 2011, p. 76)

In Italy, in 2001, the Minister of Education, University and Research set up a *Commissione ministeriale per il codice deontologico* (Ministerial Commission for the Professional Ethics Code), having a Cardinal (Ersilio Tonini) as Honorary Chair.[31] One of the Commission's conclusions was that the adoption and

---

[28] www.oas.org/cotep/LibraryDetails.aspx?lang=en&id=98.

[29] www.ncte-india.org/Approved%20by%20CP%20Final%20-%20Code%20of%20Professional%20Ethics%204%20march%202011.pdf.

[30] https://webgate.ec.europa.eu/fpfis/mwikis/eurydice/index.php/News#Launch_of_Teachers_agenda_2013-2020_in_the_Netherlands_4.12.2013.

[31] www.sissco.it//index.php?id=1180.

supervision of the respect of Professional Standards should be entrusted to the profession itself by means of a self-governing body. In its opinion, the recognition of the profession's autonomy is in line with international trends. That is why one of its "Recommendations to the Minister" was the following: to launch a process of consultation and a debate with a view to establishing a teaching profession's self-governing body similar to the existing General Teaching Councils. It could be named *Consiglio Superiore della Docenza* (Teaching High Council) and should be composed of a professional majority.

From the history of the international movement towards the teaching profession's self-regulation, some general conclusions may be drawn:

- Two conditions are determinative for the establishment and success of a teaching profession's self-governing body: professional and political will. As the Report of the Parliament of the Commonwealth of Australia (1998) read: "The establishment of such a national body is no small undertaking. It will need the goodwill of governments, teacher unions, professional subject associations and teacher training institutions" (pp. 18, 19). All stakeholders need fully to understand and value its significance and benefits.
- The establishment of self-regulation bodies was always prepared by studies of experts or commissions, and broad consultations. For example, in Ontario, the Government followed the recommendations of the *Royal Commission on Learning* and appointed the *Ontario College of Teachers Implementation Committee*. The titles of their Reports are meaningful: *For the Love of Learning* and *The Privilege of Professionalism*, respectively.
- The establishment of a teaching profession self-regulation body was a more or less lengthy process in each country, but the way paved so far allows proceeding faster nowadays.

In any case, professional self-regulation is not an "Open Sesame", i.e. an automatic solution for all of the teaching profession's problems, let alone of education. Teachers should not delude themselves nor should society expect from professional self-regulation what it cannot guarantee. On the one hand, the authority and influence of the teaching profession self-governing bodies depend on their statutory autonomy, terms of reference, composition and quality of their members. On the other hand, the accomplishment of the uniqueness and fullness of the profession calls for a right to education politics. Finland is a case in point.

In Finland, the teaching profession holds a very high status, as we know, and there is no professional self-regulation body. However, the Finish case should be regarded in light of the following:

- Professional self-regulation is not an abstract principle, like a dogma, it is a socio-economic phenomenon that is to be regarded and interpreted according to cultural and political contexts and conditions.

- Finland is one of the European countries with less professional regulation, in general,[32] and public professional self-regulation is a rarity. Advocacy is the only "liberal profession" with a statutory self-governing body.[33]
- For historical and cultural reasons and due to their high professional education level since the 1970s, Finnish teachers are highly trusted and have been closely involved in education reforms.
- More than 95 % of the Finnish teachers are members of the Trade Union of Education (OAJ), established in 1973, whose role "has been both a negotiator of the terms of teachers' employment contracts and speaker for education" (Sahlberg 2011, p. 78).[34]

7.5 Profile

The first International Conference of Teaching Councils took place in Edinburgh (Scotland), in 2005, and adopted the "Edinburgh Declaration".[35] It is a brief document in which the participants agreed, among others, to: "Promote, internationally, the highest standards and shared values of the teaching profession, in the interests of the public", while respecting "the diversity of students, pupils and teachers", and "supporting new and emerging Councils to develop appropriate models of professionally-led regulation". The second conference took place in Melbourne (Australia) in 2006 and the third in Cardiff (Wales) in 2009. The more than 50 participants in the Cardiff Conference adopted the "Cardiff Commitment", according to which:

- an International Forum should be set up,
- a "Charter for Teaching Councils" should be developed,
- the Teaching Councils should meet on an international basis biennially.

---

[32] Countries with a high degree of regulation intensity for all professions are Austria, Italy, Luxembourg and, with some exceptions in the field of technical services, Germany as well as France (and possibly Greece). Belgium and Spain (and possibly Portugal) appear to be in the medium category, whereas UK, Sweden (with the exception of pharmacists), the Netherlands, Ireland, Finland and Denmark (the latter again with the exception of pharmacists) show rather liberal regulatory regimes (at least from a comparative point of view within the EU). (http://ec.europa.eu/competition/sectors/professional_services/studies/prof_services_ihs_part_1.pdf).

[33] The Finnish Bar Association, with Public Law character, but without obligatory membership. Professional regulation is mainly a task of the National Board of Education (22 professions) and of the National Supervisory Authority for Welfare and Health (Valvira) (31 professions). Physicians, for instance, are regulated by Valvira. (www.oph.fi/english/services/recognition/regulated_professions).

[34] Paying 1.2 % of their gross salary to supporting OAJ. (www.oaj.fi/portal/page?_pageid=515,452376and_dad=portaland_schema=PORTAL).

[35] www.gtcs.org.uk/nmsruntime/saveasdialog.aspx?lID=413andsID=1008).

The International Forum of Teaching Regulatory Authorities (IFTRA) was established.[36] Its last Conference took place in 2014, in Toronto, hosted by the Ontario College of Teachers.

Two African bodies—Teachers Registration Council of Nigeria (TRCN) and South African Council for Educators (SACE)—organized the "1st Roundtable of Teaching Regulatory Authorities in Africa", in Abuja, Nigeria, in 2010, whose theme was "The Role of the African Nations in the Globalisation of the Teaching Profession".[37] It adopted the following agreements, in particular:

1. There should be a law establishing Teachers Regulatory Authority (TRA) in each African country.
[…]
8. The African Roundtable be institutionalised and to hold annually.

The Africa Forum for Teaching Regulatory Authorities (AFTRA) was also established. Its roundtables following the first one in Nigeria (2010) took place in South Africa (2011), Tanzania (2012), Kenya (2013) and Ghana (2014).

A Charter for Teaching Councils was adopted. Here is its full text[38]:

Charter for Teaching Councils

This Charter has been drawn up by the associate councils[39] that comprise the International Forum for Teacher Regulatory Authorities. Its purpose is to gather together the typical benefits, purposes and functions of Teaching Councils so that policy makers and those with an interest in promoting teacher professionalism and strengthening teacher accountability internationally can draw from the experience of existing councils to promote best practice globally and to assist in the establishment of new Councils.

Purpose

Teaching Councils usually have three allied purposes:

- To improve standards of teaching and learning in their jurisdictions,
- To raise the standing of the teaching profession, and
- To assure the public of the conduct and competence of teachers.

Benefits

- Higher standards of teacher conduct and competence,
- Improved learning outcomes for children and young people,
- Higher levels of public trust and confidence in the teaching profession,
- Improved self-esteem of teachers through association with a professional regulatory body,
- Clear accountability for Professional Standards and conduct.

---

[36] www.iftra.org.

[37] www.trcn.gov.ng/aftra/1st_doc/AFTRA_communique.pdf.

[38] www.senedd.assemblywales.org/documents/s20291/Consultation%20Response%20EB% 2017%20General%20Teaching%20Council%20for%20Wales.pdf.

[39] "Teaching Councils" is used consistently in this Charter to describe the functions and purposes of bodies that may have other titles, such as a Teacher Registration Board or a College of Teachers.

Functions

The functions carried out by teaching councils include the following:

- Maintaining a register of those qualified and fit to practise,
- Advising on or establishing Professional Standards/competences for entry to the profession,
- Ensuring that registered teachers meet the expected standards,
- Setting standards for, advising on, and monitoring programmes of initial teacher education,
- Setting standards for, advising on, monitoring or making provision for teachers' continuing professional development,
- Commissioning, facilitating or undertaking research into effective practice.

These functions are usually discharged by:

- Publishing a code of ethics/conduct/practice,
- Investigating and adjudicating on the fitness to practise of individual teachers including their professional conduct and/or competence,
- Drawing upon research and evidence to advise policy makers and service providers on effective policies to improve standards of teaching and learning,
- Assessing the suitability of those who wish to train as teachers,
- Maintaining a register which may include different categories of registration, according to practitioners' qualifications,
- The accreditation of initial teacher education courses.

Founding Principles that Distinguish Teaching Councils

- Teaching Councils work first and foremost for the common good and in the public interest,
- Teaching Councils have an established statutory and legal basis,
- Teaching Councils are independent of government direction,
- Teaching Councils promote the teaching profession rather than the interests of individual teachers,
- Teaching Councils promote professionally led regulation.

The Most Effective Teaching Councils

- Command the respect of the public and the profession,
- Are the pivotal agency for governments on teaching quality,
- Enhance teacher professionalism by raising standards of practice and improving initial and continuing education,
- Maintain and make public an accurate register of teachers' qualification status and fitness to practice.

Another way of articulating the vision of the logic, fullness and sense of a teaching profession's self-governing body could be as follows:

- *Purposes*

  - To personify the identity of the teaching profession.
  - To care about teachers' professionalism.
  - To raise public confidence in the profession and education quality.

- *Principles*

  – Statutory autonomy.
  – Primacy of the public interest.
  – Benefits of professional self-regulation for all stakeholders.

- *Powers and functions*

  – Registration and certification of the profession's membership.
  – Investigation and sanction of breaches of Professional Standards.
  – Adoption or participation in approval of Professional Standards for:

    - initial and continuing education,
    - certification/recertification,
    - professional practice and conduct.

  – Accreditation and/or supervision of initial and continuing education programmes.
  – Dissemination of information of interest to the members of the profession, by all appropriate means.
  – Initiative/sponsorship of research and publications on professional matters.
  – Advice and recommendations on issues within the scope of its mandate.
  – Representation of the profession concerning its most general interests.
  – Other powers, functions and activities, such as:

    - promotion and organization of programmes of professional development;
    - supervision of professional induction/probation and role of appeal body with regard to the evaluation of this;
    - recognition of professional qualifications acquired out of its jurisdiction, especially in federal states;
    - creation of the committees/commissions necessary for the exercise of its powers and functions, with possible recourse to experts outside of the profession.

- *Very high profile professional self-regulation*

  – Self-regulatory body with statutory autonomy, a professional majority and an elected Chair/Director.
  – Jurisdiction over the whole education professions, both in the public and in the private sectors, including preschool education and higher education.
  – Broad mandate, in addition to registration and certification, including accreditation of professional education and disciplinary power.
  – Authority recognized and respected by the profession, by the public and by Governments.

References

Asia Society. (2013). *The 2013 international summit on the teaching profession—Teacher quality.* http://asiasociety.org/files/teachingsummit2013.pdf

Carr, D. (2000). *Professionalism and ethics in teaching.* London, New York: Routledge (reprinted 2004).

House of Commons. (2012). *Great teachers: attracting, training and retaining the best. Ninth report of session 2010–12 (Vol. I). Report, together with formal minutes great teachers: Attracting, training and retaining the best ninth report of session 2010–12.* London: Education Committee. www.publications.parliament.uk/pa/cm201012/cmselect/cmeduc/1515/1515.pdf

ILO. (2012). *Handbook of good human resource practices in the teaching profession.* Geneva: Sectoral Activities Department, International Labour Organization. www.ilo.org/wcmsp5/groups/public/—ed_dialogue/—sector/documents/publication/wcms_187793.pdf

Irish National Teachers' Organisation. (1992). *Professionalism in the 1990s.* Dublin: Irish National Teachers' Organisation. www.into.ie/ROI/Publications/PublicationsPre2000/Professionalisminthe1990s_1992.pdf

Irish National Teachers' Organization. (1994). *Comhairle Muinteoireachta—A Teaching Council,* Dublin. www.into.ie/ROI/Publications/PublicationsPre2000/ATeachingCouncil1994.pdf

Kendel, D. (2013). *For the sake of students—A report prepared by Dr. Dennis Kendel on current and future teacher regulation in the province of Saskatchewan.* http://education.gov.sk.ca/educator-services/regulation/for-the-sake-of-students.pdf

Leslie, Ch. (Ed.). (2013). *Towards a royal college of teaching—Raising the status of the profession.* London: The Royal College of Surgeons of England. Retrieved July 2014, from http://filestore.aqa.org.uk/news/pdf/AQA-NEWS-TOWARDS-A-ROYAL-COLLEGE.PDF

MacBeath, J. (2012). *Future of teaching profession.* Education International Research Institute, University of Cambridge, Leadership for Learning, The Cambridge Network. http://download.ei-ie.org/Docs/WebDepot/EI%20Study%20on%20the%20Future%20of%20Teaching%20Profession.pdf

OECD. (2005). *Teachers matter—Attracting, developing and retaining effective teachers.* OECD Publishing.

Parliament of the Commonwealth of Australia. (1998). *A Class Act—Inquiry into the status of the teaching profession.* Canberra: Senate Employment, Education and Training Reference Committee. www.aph.gov.au/~/media/wopapub/senate/committee/eet_ctte/completed_inquiries/1996_99/teachers/report/report_pdf.ashx

Ramsey, G. (2000). *Quality matters—Revitalising teaching: Critical times, critical choices—Report of the Review of Teacher Education,* New South Wales. www.det.nsw.edu.au/teachrev/reports/reports.pdf

Sahlberg, P. (2011). *Finnish lessons: What can the world learn from educational change in Finland.* New York: Teachers College Press.

Saskatchewan Teachers' Federation. (2013). *Teacher professionalism in Saskatchewan strengthening regulation.* www.stf.sk.ca/portal.jsp?Sy3uQUnbK9L2RmSZs02CjV3Jh9YwRCfE6pk95yAgweQU=F

Sayer, J. (2000). *The General Teaching Council.* London, New York: Cassell.

Schratz, M. (2011). Professionalität und Professionalisierung von Lehrerinnen und Lehrern in internationaler Perspektive (Professionality and Professionalization of Teachers in International Perspective). In M. Schratz et al. (Hg.), *Pädagogishe Professionalität: quer denken, umdenken, neu denken—Impulse für next practice im Lehrerberuf* (pp. 46–94). Wien: Facultas Verlag- und Buchandels AG.

Sexton, M. (2007). Evaluating teaching as a profession—Implications of a research study for the work of the teaching council. *Irish Education Studies, 26*(1), 79–105.

Tardif, M., & Gauthier, C. (Dir.). (1999). *Pour ou contre un ordre professionnel des enseignantes et des enseignants au Québec.* Québec: Les Presses de l'Université Laval.

Thompson, M. (1997). *Professional ethics and the teacher—Towards a general teaching council.* Oakhill: Trentham Books.

Towsley, L. (1991). *A work of justice and progress—The story of the UNESCO/ILO 1966 recommendation concerning the status of teachers.* Morges, Switzerland: World Confederation of Organizations of the Teaching Profession.

UNESCO. (1998). *World education report—1998—Teachers and teaching in a changing world.* www.unesco.org/education/information/wer/PDFeng/wholewer98.PDF

Van Nuland, Sh. (1998). *The development of the Ontario College of Teachers.* Toronto: University of Toronto. Retrieved January 2013 from https://tspace.library.utoronto.ca/handle/1807/12402

Willis, R. (2005). *The struggle for the General Teaching Council.* New York: RoutledgeFalmer.

Chapter 8
Conclusion

Abstract The human species is essentially educable because of its biological perfectibility, which is the source of its cultural creativity and the ground of its ethical dignity. That is why a human being is able to ascend to sublimity and descend to cruelty of which no other animal is capable. Education may be considered the greatest human power and responsibility. How might it cease being largely an incestuous cloning of older generations into the coming ones, hindering the perfecting of Humankind? The Gordian Knot of Humankind having to educate itself—and of the vicious circle of the reproduction of education's wrongs—will only begin to be disentangled when its children may learn how to be with loving and enlightened parents, as well as with education professionals chosen among the best human beings and educated to act illuminated by the highest human values and the best knowledge. As a consequence, professional exemplarity, rightly understood, may be considered the quintessence of the teaching profession. In no other profession is example so essential and central. Professional self-regulation is a privilege teachers should strive for, a power they should be able to have, and a responsibility they should deserve. It may be a royal route to higher professionality, i.e. to superior identity and dignity, with the potential to become a bridge between the present and the future of the teaching profession.

Keywords Human educability · Gordian knot · Professional exemplarity · Professional self-regulation

The truth about human nature is that we are what our genetic heritage, living conditions and education make of us. Each human being becomes the result of his or her striving for life, drive for recognition and whole education.

The human species is essentially educable because of its biological perfectibility, which is the source of its cultural creativity and the ground of its ethical dignity. That is why a human being is able to ascend to sublimity and descend to cruelty of which no other animal is capable.

© The Author(s) 2015
A. Reis Monteiro, *The Teaching Profession*, SpringerBriefs in Education,
DOI 10.1007/978-3-319-12130-7_8

The Little Prince[1] began his interplanetary journey—"in order to add to his knowledge"—by visiting the asteroid 325, inhabited by a king "who felt consumingly proud of being at last a king over somebody". What the king "fundamentally insisted upon was that his authority should be respected. He tolerated no disobedience", because he was an absolute, but reasonable, monarch. "I have the right to require obedience because my orders are reasonable". Consequently, as the fifth planet's lamplighter said: "There is nothing to understand. Orders are orders". However: "That is the tragedy! From year to year the planet has turned more rapidly and the orders have not been changed!"

Education may be considered the greatest human power and responsibility. How might it cease being largely an incestuous cloning of older generations into the coming ones, by means of *orders* hindering the perfecting of the Humankind?

The Gordian Knot of Humankind having to educate itself—and of the vicious circle of the reproduction of education's wrongs—will only begin to be disentangled when its children may learn how to be with loving and enlightened parents, as well as with education professionals chosen among the best human beings and educated to act illuminated by the highest human values and the best knowledge.

For children, their parents are unique in the world, but they may not be the best persons of the world. They are not chosen, but they can learn to love and educate their children with respect for their equal human dignity and rights. Furthermore, education professionals may be chosen and educated to act on behalf of Humankind that "owes to each child the best it has to give" (in French: *l'humanité se doit de donner à l'enfant le meilleur d'elle-même*), as the Declaration of the Rights of the Child (United Nations, 1959)[2] proclaims in the last paragraph of its Preamble. These words, taken from the 1924 Geneva Declaration of the Rights of the Child,[3] have been kept out of the 1989 United Nations Convention on the Rights of the Child,[4] but may be considered the loveliest and noblest words of International Human Rights Law.

As Lee Iacocca (a famous American businessman) said: "In a truly rational society, the best of us would be teachers, and the rest would have to settle for something less" (as cit. in National Commission on Teaching and America's Future 1996, p. 24).[5] Indeed, in education, there is no professional quality without personal quality. No "collaborative culture" or "learning community" is able to skip the unique educational resonance of a teacher's personality. In no other profession is example so essential and central. Professional exemplarity, rightly understood, may be considered the quintessence of the teaching profession.

However, there is often a general chronic recklessness of the silent but profound resonance the teachers' personalities may have into the lives of their students, as if

---

[1] http://cs.swan.ac.uk/~cswill/The_little_prince.pdf.

[2] www.un.org/cyberschoolbus/humanrights/resources/child.asp.

[3] www.un-documents.net/gdrc1924.htm.

[4] www.unesco.org/education/pdf/CHILD_E.PDF.

[5] http://nctaf.org/wp-content/uploads/WhatMattersMost.pdf.

who the teacher is had nothing or little to do with *what he or she does*. Whatever the difficulties in selecting the best, one must not lose sight of what is at stake. The Royal Commission on Learning (1995),[6] in Ontario, highlighted it clearly: *We believe that the right of children to a good education is the most important consideration* (italics original, p. 295).

Professional self-regulation allows for teachers to assume the cultivation of the value and values of their profession, if the teaching profession's self-governing bodies represent the best it has to give and act inspired by a vision of its uniqueness and fullness. In this respect, let us recall what the aforementioned Royal Commission on Learning (1995) recommended: "The Commission believes that the teaching profession in Ontario must now be considered equal to other established professions. [...] Giving teaching full professional status is a logical extension of trends in education and developments in the teaching community". Accordingly, it recommended:

> 58. That a professional self-regulatory body for teaching, the Ontario College of Teachers, be established, with the powers, duties, and membership of the College set out in legislation. The College should be responsible for determining professional standards, certification, and accreditation of teacher education programs. Professional educators should form a majority of the membership of the College, with substantial representation of non-educators from the community at large;
>
> 59. That the College of Teachers, in close co-operation with faculties of education, develop a framework for accrediting teacher preparation programs offered by Ontario faculties of education, and that the College be responsible for carrying out such accreditation processes;
>
> 60. That faculties of education and school staff who supervise student teachers be accountable for ensuring that those recommended for Ontario Teaching Certificates have the qualities required for admission to the teaching profession, and that those candidates who do not show such qualities be advised to leave teacher preparation programs; (pp. 282, 284, 293, 295)

Education and the teaching profession have nothing to lose but much to gain with professional self-regulation. It may have decisive repercussions on the vision of the identity and attractiveness of the profession; on the selection, education and evaluation of teachers; on their professional and social status, self-esteem and motivation; on the mission of school as an institution of humanization; and on the quality of education as a human right and a public and global good.

Professional self-regulation is a privilege teachers should strive for, a power they should be able to have and a responsibility they should deserve. It may be a royal route to higher professionality, i.e. to superior identity and dignity, with the potential to become a bridge between the present and future of the teaching profession.

---

[6] www.edu.gov.on.ca/eng/general/abcs/rcom/full/royalcommission.pdf.

References

National Commission on Teaching and America's Future. (1996). *What matters most: Teaching for America's future*. New York.

Royal Commission on Learning. (1995). *For the love of learning*. www.edu.gov.on.ca/eng/general/abcs/rcom/full/royalcommission.pdf

Appendix—Summary

A.1 Introduction

Quality education is a leitmotif of political-pedagogical rhetoric, both at the international and national levels. The most decisive ingredient of education quality is the quality of the teaching profession—this is a main finding of numerous international and national reports and studies on the teaching profession and education systems published during the last three decades or so. However, another equally main finding is that the overall teachers' status, in most countries, is low or very low.

How then to conceive of and achieve quality in the teaching profession? Given its degraded status and the revolution of technologies of information and communication, another issue is emerging: Does the teaching profession have a future?

These and other related questions are succinctly addressed in the three parts of this volume.

A.2 Main Approaches to Education Quality

Classic pedagogic thought is concerned with *good education*. Since the 1980s, however, *quality education* has become the watchword. What exactly is 'quality' in education?

We may distinguish two principal approaches: the human capital approach and the human rights approach. The human capital approach to education quality is supported by a neoliberal conception of the school's mission and of the identity of the teaching profession, based on quasi-market principles. The human rights approach to education quality is inspired by the normative content of the right to education, as internationally agreed, reflecting human rights values and principles.

Quality education is a complex concept, with material and non-material dimensions, resulting from the interaction between tangible and intangible ingredients. While there is no recipe or ready-to-wear approach to producing

© The Author(s) 2015
A. Reis Monteiro, *The Teaching Profession*, SpringerBriefs in Education,
DOI 10.1007/978-3-319-12130-7

quality education, there are principles universally valid and applicable, forming a common pedagogic heritage of Humankind amply consecrated by the Ethics of the Right to Education. In addition, every country can learn from the most exemplary ones.

A.3 Most Far-Reaching Lessons from Studies, Reforms and Reports Concerning Education Systems and the Teaching Profession Worldwide

The human species being essentially perfectible and educable, the primacy of education is a recurrent theme in the classic sources of pedagogic thought. It has been endowed with the status of a human right, and *key* is a word often used to indicate the paramountcy of the right to education.

Nevertheless, while it is largely recognised that education is the great 'social equalizer' and that achieving both educational 'excellence' and 'equity' is one of the most critical problems of our times, education systems are not keeping up with increasingly multicultural and rapidly changing societies. They need radical reforms. A reform is not radical enough if it does not grasp the roots of what is failing. In addition, it must be systemic, holistic, taking into account the interaction of education with the whole society since human rights are essentially indivisible and interdependent.

Although teachers are the real genius of the everyday alchemy of education quality, two terms are frequently used with respect to the status of the teaching profession worldwide: 'decline' and (lack of) 'recognition'. The minimum that may be said is that it is uncared for: it is uncared for when Governments do not care for it and it does not care for itself. The quality of the teaching profession is neither cheap nor evaluable in snapshot, but what is at stake in education is priceless.

Finland's education system is example of a human rights approach to education quality, driven by a highly qualified and ranked teaching profession. It epitomizes the compatibility between equity and quality, inclusiveness and competitiveness, thus making more evident, by contrast, how miserable neoliberal education politics is.

A.4 Sociology of the Professions

The Sociology of the Professions is a domain within the Sociology of Work whose object is the study of professions as a special category of occupations. The distinction between 'profession' and 'occupation'—its Anglo-Saxon starting point—is thus understood: While the term 'occupation' means every activity, work, function or job that is the main source of someone's livelihood, the term 'profession' distinguishes a more or less specialized, well-paid and prestigious occupation.

The main approaches and theories in the field of the Sociology of the Professions are the following: functionalist ('trait approach'), interactionist ('process approach') and conflict ('power approach').

I submit that every lawful occupation, by means of which individuals earn their principal regular income, is their profession, with its corresponding utility and dignity, whatever its reality. Nevertheless, while a case may be made for considering the distinction between profession and occupation as a socially elitist construct, there are objective differences and social differentiation among occupations/professions.

Occupations distinguish themselves by their level of professionality (or professionhood). Professionalism is a more frequently used word, but their distinction and definitions are not well-established in the sociological literature. As understood here, professionality means the global profile of a profession, that is, everything distinguishing it from other occupational groups; professionalism means the practice of a profession according to its identity content, as described in Professional Standards. Ultimately, professionalism amounts to the unity of science, conscience and excellence.

Professional Standards are principally standards for professional fitness, competence, education, practice and conduct. They should form the normative framework essential for accreditation of initial and continuing education, for registration and certification, for any possible disciplinary sanction, as well as for the periodic evaluation of performance.

Another relevant sociological concept is that of professional self-regulation. It will be the focus of the third part of this study.

A.5 Teaching as a Profession

According to international and national reports and studies, the overall status of the teaching profession is not very prestigious (and indeed far from it), as already mentioned. Underlying its widely degraded status—and being decisive for its future —is the *crux* of grasping its very identity.

Teachers should consider themselves and be considered as professionals of the right to education and of pedagogic communication, the center of gravity of their professionalism being interpersonal relationship.

At the core of the teaching profession is its unique and far-reaching ethical dimension. The improvement of its quality should therefore begin at … the beginning. The human quality of the candidates to exercising the profession should be taken into account when deciding on the criteria for entering professional education and evaluating professional performance.

Besides selection, education and evaluation, improving the quality of the teaching profession should also include other aspects of its professional and social status, such as working conditions, as well as pay and career perspectives, without overlooking the relevance of school management.

The future of the teaching profession is obviously tied to that of the school. Teachers should become professionals of example. Professional exemplarity should be understood as an exceptional incarnation of a blend of qualities, values and knowledge.

The teaching profession should be principally responsible for attracting the best human beings to their profession. How? By means of outstanding professional self-governing bodies, i.e. composed of people holding a passionate and inspiring vision.

A.6 Regulation of Professions

Professional self-regulation is a hallmark of the most socially relevant, responsible and recognized professions. It is the gold standard of professional status in most Anglo-Saxon countries but, in the rest of the world, it has not been favoured by the centralized Nation-States.

Economic regulation means State intervention in the domain of economic-professional activities, in the public interest, that is, to protect consumers, clients and society in general from potential harm.

Professional regulation basically consists in controlling the access to the practice of a profession by means of registration and certification or licensure, aiming at assuring that professionals provide services in a competent, ethical and safe manner, with the highest quality and at an affordable price.

Professional self-regulation means, literally, the regulation of a profession by itself. It may be purely private, private but with some kind of official recognition, or public. It is public when operated by a professional body vested with statutory powers delegated by the Legislature. The basic self-regulatory powers and functions are registration and certification or licensure of the profession's members. The highest and most arduous mission of a self-regulatory body is adopting, cultivating and supervising respect for Professional Standards. Its supreme empowerment is the disciplinary one, which amounts to a judicial power.

Professional self-regulation is sometimes objected to chiefly for the following reasons: it lacks democratic legitimacy; it is incompatible with freedom of association; it is inherently exposed to a potential conflict of interests; it is an obstacle to competition. Such objections either have no valid foundation or may be solved. Professional self-regulation brings benefits for all stakeholders. They may be summarized in four 'Ps': public, professional, personal and political.

Could the teaching profession be self-governing? What can teachers win with it?

A.7 Self-regulation of the Teaching Profession

The teaching profession's self-regulation already exists in several Anglo-Saxon countries. The general term for its bodies is 'Teaching Council'. The first one was created in Scotland in 1965, but most now existing were established during the first decade of the 21st century. Australia is where they most recently and quickly expanded. The General Teaching Council for Scotland and the Ontario College of Teachers are high profile and have been the most influential in the establishment of other similar bodies, which have varied designations and self-regulatory profiles. In the rest of the world, the regulation of the teaching profession is generally carried out by States, either directly or by means of a special Agency/Authority.

If the teaching profession's self-regulation continues to be exceptional world-wide, it is because it meets with resistances, which are chiefly political and/or trade unionist. A strong argument, among others, in favor of it is a matter of fact: it already exists and keeps expanding worldwide. A Charter for Teaching Councils was adopted.

In sum: There is no fully true profession without a professional entity—crossing its associative diversity—that should be the *Body* of its unity, the *Face* of its identity, the *Voice* of its authority, the *Guardian* of its integrity, the *Prophet* of its future.

In any case, professional self-regulation is not an 'Open Sesame', i.e. an automatic solution for all of the teaching profession's problems, let alone of education.

A.8 Conclusion

The human species is essentially educable because of its biological perfectibility, which is the source of its cultural creativity and the ground of its ethical dignity. That is why a human being is able to ascend to sublimity and descend to cruelty of which no other animal is capable.

Education may be considered the greatest human power and responsibility. How might it cease being largely an incestuous cloning of older generations into the coming ones, hindering the perfecting of the Humankind?

The Gordian Knot of Humankind having to educate itself—and of the vicious circle of the reproduction of education's wrongs—will only begin to be disentangled when its children may learn how to be with loving and enlightened parents, as well as with education professionals chosen among the best human beings and educated to act illuminated by the highest human values and the best knowledge.

As a consequence, professional exemplarity, rightly understood, may be considered the quintessence of the teaching profession. In no other profession is example so essential and central.

Professional self-regulation is a privilege teachers should strive for, a power they should be able to have, and a responsibility they should deserve. It may be a royal route to higher professionality, i.e. to superior identity and dignity, with the potential to become a bridge between the present and the future of the teaching profession.